THOMAS BOSTON
A Heart for Service

ANDREW THOMSON

CHRISTIAN FOCUS

First Published as
THOMAS BOSTON OF ETTRICK:
HIS LIFE AND TIMES
by
Rev. Andrew Thomson, D.D., F.R.S.E.

Thomson(1814 -1901) was minister of Broughton Place United Presbyterian Kirk, Edinburgh. His other books include *John Owen, Prince of Puritans*(ISBN 1-85792-267-0) and *Richard Baxter, The Pastor's Pastor*(ISBN 1-85792-380-4).

ISBN 1-85792-379-0

This edition published in 2004
by
Christian Focus Publications Ltd.
Geanies House, Fearn, Tain,
Ross-shire, IV20 ITW, Great Britain

www.christianfocus.com

Printed and bound by AIT Nørhaven A/S, Denmark

Cover design by Alister MacInnes

CONTENTS

FOREWORD TO THE NEW EDITION

Introduction

It is good at last to have Andrew Thomson's biography of Thomas Boston back in print. There has been some considerable attention given to Boston's theology over recent years, both at an academic and a popular level, but little or nothing of a biographical nature has been written. There is room indeed for a critical, intellectual biography. Thomson's work, of course, is not of that nature but is rather a typical product of its nineteenth century origins. The language is somewhat quaint and old fashioned but it is not a barrier to understanding and is appropriate to its context, coming as it does from a day when a more formal and elaborate writing style was common.

The question which must be answered, however, is why we ought to be grateful for the republication of this biography. In other words, what is it about the life and ministry of Thomas Boston that justifies this publication? To answer this question it is useful to look at the various aspects of his life and ministry.

Boston the Man

In seeking to understand Thomas Boston, we are fortunate in having not only this biography by Andrew Thomson but also Boston's own autobiography, written for his children. The picture that emerges is of a serious man but a man with a warm and compassionate heart. He did have a somewhat introspective personality and was rather hard on himself both physically and spiritually. Physically, it showed itself in a number of ways, not least in his regular spells of prayer and fasting. Another example comes from his days as a student in Edinburgh, when he was so concerned at the cost of his studies to his father that he practically starved himself and made himself ill. Spiritually, the introspection led him to a sharp analysis of his own spiritual condition, an attitude which stands in marked contrast to the rather superficial spirituality of much of today's church. Occasionally he might be thought to have gone a little far, however, such as the time he rebuked himself for lying a little longer in bed on a Monday morning after a busy Lord's Day and chastised himself for 'sleeping away the blessing'!

His family life was not without great difficulties. He and his wife had several children who died in infancy and the pain of these experiences is evident in his writing. He himself suffered ill health for most of his life but this was as nothing compared to the suffering of his wife who was mentally ill for most of their married life. The care and tenderness which he showed towards her was a model to others. Even when he was dying, he was concerned to ensure that his children would take proper care of her after he had gone. Despite much suffering, however, he was blessed in many ways, not least in seeing his children follow Christ. Indeed, at the last communion service he took in Ettrick, it was his great joy to see the last of his children come to the table.

Boston the Minister

Thomas Boston (1676–1732) was a minister of the Church of Scotland who served in the Scottish border country, first in the parish of Simprin and then, for the remainder of his ministry, in the parish of Ettrick. He was a gifted and dedicated minister whose devotion to the tasks he believed God had committed to him was an example to others. This consisted primarily of the pastoral care of his flock, including the practice of catechising, and the work of preaching and teaching. It is clear that Boston could be rather stern and judgemental, especially in his earlier years but his love and compassion for his flock were also self-evident.

He was a convinced Presbyterian and played his part in the wider life of the denomination, not least by serving for a time as Clerk to the Synod. He was unswerving in his commitment to the

Church of Scotland, the established church, even being willing to take an undeserved rebuke from the General Assembly over the *Marrow* controversy. He died before some of the other *Marrowmen* left the Kirk to form the First Secession Church but it is clear from his writings, especially on the evils of schism, that he would not have followed them.

Boston the Preacher

Boston's early preaching tended to be very legal, warning people of the demands of God's law and the consequences of breaking it, but an older, wiser minister once told him to stop 'railing' at his people and to preach grace. This he did and his ministry was transformed. Indeed, we might describe Boston as a preacher of grace in the midst of a context where legalism was present in much of Scottish preaching.

We are fortunate in having many volumes of his sermons available to us and so we can see what he gave to his people. There is a depth both of content and of spirituality which shines out from these sermons. Thomson rightly describes the seriousness with which Boston took this responsibility and describes how he would spend time before the Lord before ever he would go over to the church to preach, emphasising his complete dependence upon the work of the Holy Spirit. His congregation was given solid meat and there are many so-called educated congregations today who would struggle to follow his teaching and take in all that he said. This is a reflection on our present ignorance rather than on Boston, for his people were steeped in the Scriptures and in the Shorter Catechism and for that reason many of them were better theologians than some who occupy pulpits today. Thomson himself notes that those who had heard Boston preach the two volumes of sermons on the Shorter Catechism were well equipped to debate with any of the ministers even of that day!

His normal practice was to extract some doctrine from the text and to apply it to his hearers. His sermons were very carefully structured and hence easier for his people to remember. There was also a passion and a pathos about his preaching, which was blessed by God to the salvation of many. The story of Boston's last few sermons, some of them preached from an armchair specially put into the pulpit when he could no longer stand and the remainder preached from an open window in the manse, bear witness both to his faithfulness to his calling and to the desire in the hearts of his congregation to hear yet another sermon from this godly, dying man.

Boston the Controversialist

Boston was not one of those who relish argument and controversy and are always seeking some issue on which to do battle but, once he had reached a position on a matter, he was willing to stand his ground. For example, when Professor Simson of Glasgow University was charged with heresy and the General Assembly took an incredibly lenient view of the matter (in contrast with its later treatment of the *Marrowmen*), Boston was prepared to stand alone in the Assembly, in order to protest and complain against the decision. This was not easy for him because he was not one of life's natural controversialists and he was very unhappy when some others then tried to use this protest for their own ends, being afraid lest people might think that he was party to the action.

The major controversy in which Boston was involved was the *Marrow* controversy. A book, *The Marrow of Modern Divinity*, was published in 1645. The name of the author was withheld and he was simply identified by the initials 'EF'. It is now generally agreed that this was Edward Fisher. Although he was the 'author' of the book (in two volumes), in fact the book is mostly made up of quotations from many of the best Reformed writers, such as Calvin and Rutherford. Fisher took and used the 'marrow' or the 'core' of their writings, hence the title. Much of it consists of a dialogue between various characters, including an antinomian (one who believed that the law had no significance for Christians), a neonomian (legalist) and a minister of the gospel. It is very cleverly written and is a powerful presentation of the gospel.

Boston had discovered the book in a house in Simprin and quickly encouraged his friends to read it. He later had it republished with his own notes. The prevailing party in the Church of Scotland at that time, however, believed that the book was contrary to sound doctrine and a significant controversy and pamphlet war ensued between those who were advocates of the book, the so-called *Marrowmen*, and those who were opposed to it. The theological issues at stake were the free and universal offer of the gospel, the doctrine of repentance, whether assurance was of the essence of saving faith and so on. Essentially, the *Marrowmen* were protesting against the legalism of many of their colleagues in the church. This debate culminated at the General Assembly of the Church of Scotland in 1720 when the book was 'banned', in the sense that ministers were instructed not to use it, nor to encourage anyone to read it. Even in those days it was highly unusual for a book to be treated in this way by a Protestant church.

Naturally the *Marrowmen* protested this decision and the matter rumbled on for two more years. Ultimately, however, they were rebuked by the General Assembly of 1722, although no action was taken against them in respect of their status as ministers of the Kirk nor were they removed from their congregations. Boston was at the heart of the debate over these years and the theological ability he demonstrated in presenting the arguments of the *Marrowmen* was widely respected.

Boston the Scholar

Boston was also a writer and scholar of some ability. His collected writings were published in twelve volumes in 1853.[1] The majority of his writings are sermons which he preached in Ettrick, although he also published a number of little books, including *The Crook in the Lot*. The most famous of his writings is *Human Nature in its Fourfold State* in which he developed almost a complete systematic theology by considering the various stages through which humanity has passed: man in innocence (before the Fall), man in sin (post-Fall), man saved (the Christian state) and man in glory (the future state of believers).

1. They have subsequently been republished twice: (Wheaton, IL: Richard Owen Roberts, 1980) and (Lafayette, IN: Sovereign Grace Publishers, 2001). They are also available from Tentmaker Publications, Stoke-on-Trent, England.

When the *Marrow of Modern Divinity* was re-published with notes by Boston, this not only helped to clarify the issues at stake in the controversy but it also helped to establish his reputation as a theologian. When his *A View of the Covenant of* Works and *A View of the Covenant of Grace* were published, he was reckoned to be one of the finest exponents of covenant theology, even being compared to Witsius and other giants. His manuscript of *Miscellaneous Questions* gives a good picture of a man wrestling with some of the great theological issues and doing so without the resources available to scholars today. His library was very small indeed. It was not only in systematic theology, however, that his reputation was made. He was a Hebrew scholar of the first rank, in communication with Hebrew scholars all over Europe. His book on the Hebrew accents argued a case which proved to be wrong but even the ability to argue such a sustained position demonstrated his supreme ability and fluency in the language. He was also competent in Latin and Greek, like most scholars of his day. Unlike some, however, he was competent in French and Thomson tells us that he could translate Dutch.

Conclusion

All that has been said so far underlines the importance and significance of Thomas Boston in the early 18th century and no doubt justifies the republication of this biography by Andrew Thomson, lest we forget one of the great men of the past. Is Boston's usefulness, then, simply historical? Or does he have significance for today?

It seems to me that a recovery of interest in Thomas Boston would be of enormous benefit for the church in our day, not least for his own Church of Scotland. There are indeed many aspects of Boston's life and ministry which we would do well to recover for our own day: his love for Christ, his concern for personal holiness, his strong evangelistic zeal for the lost, his deep pastoral concern for believers and so on. This is to say nothing of the need in our day to recover his Calvinistic, covenant theology, in a day when the Reformed heritage which has been passed down from generation to generation of Scots, since the Reformation of 1560, seems set to be lost, even among those who claim to be evangelicals. Above all, we need to recover the example Boston set as the pastor-scholar, one who took seriously his calling to be a teaching elder, as demonstrated by the seriousness with which he set about the business of preparing to preach.

As Thomson says, Boston was a truly great man. There have been few like him in our history. May God raise up more like him to assist the church in its great need today.

> Professor A. T. B. McGowan
> Highland Theological College

PREFACE

We shall not be charged with superfluous authorship in having written the following Memoir of Mr. Boston of Ettrick.[1] Nearly a century and a half has elapsed since the death of that remarkable man, and anything approaching to a complete biography of him has up to this time remained to be written.

Brief narratives regarding some of the salient points in his life, and estimates of his character, have indeed appeared at intervals, usually attached to some of his works when they were republished; but we are not aware of any book which, beginning with his early youth, and giving ample space to family incidents, has traced the story of his life through all its changeful periods – described his conflicts with surrounding errors, his influence on the condition of the church and the religious thought of his times – producing, in fact, what we mean by a biography.

No doubt we have Mr. Boston's diary, which was written by him for his family and published soon after his death, and must be invaluable to any biographer; but even it contains many gaps which need to be filled up from other sources; and besides this, it would not serve the ends of biography to be always looking at the subject of it through his eyes. We have endeavoured, in the following pages, to include in our narrative the whole range of his life and ministry; with what measure of success it will be for the intelligent and candid reader to judge.

Even in so brief a preface as this, we cannot refrain from mentioning the names of friends to whom we are conscious of owing a debt of gratitude for kindly advice and cheering

---

1. These comments were made in 1895.

encouragement in connection with the writing of this memoir. We owe a warm tribute of thanks to the Rev. John Lawson of Selkirk, who guided us for several days amid the classic scenes of Ettrick and Yarrow, and showed us sacred spots that were linked with the honoured name of the author of the 'Fourfold State'; and to Mrs. Dr. Smith of Biggar, who possesses, and kindly allowed us to photograph a portion of, the original manuscript of that work. We have also to thank our long-tried friend and fellow-labourer in the gospel, Dr. Blair of Dunblane, who was in full sympathy with us in our veneration for Mr. Boston, and ever ready with friendly advice and suggestion out of his well-stored mind. Nor can we omit to mention the name of W. White-Millar, Esq., S.S.C., the cherished friend of a long life, who grudged neither time nor trouble in procuring for us desired information on the subjects of our narrative, and in this way, as well as by his cheerful countenance, turned our labour into a pleasure. And not least do we place on grateful record our deep sense of the spiritual benefit we have derived from the study, for so many months, of the life and character of a man of the true apostolic stamp, who would have been justly regarded as a star of the first magnitude, an ornament to the Christian Church even in the brightest and purest periods of its history.

1

INTRODUCTION

It would be difficult to name a man who has a higher claim to an honourable place in the Christian biography of Scotland in the eighteenth century than Thomas Boston of Ettrick. We deem it sufficient of itself to explain and justify this statement, that he was the author of the 'Fourfold State'. It is a remarkable circumstance that, from the days of the Reformation downward, there has always been some one book in which the vitalizing element has been peculiarly strong, and which God has singled out as the instrument of almost innumerable conversions, as well as of quickening and deepening the divine life in those who had already believed. Luther's 'Commentary on Galatians', Baxter's 'Call to the Unconverted', Bunyan's 'Pilgrim's Progress', Alleine's 'Alarm', Doddridge's 'Rise and Progress', Fuller's 'Great Question Answered', Wilberforce's 'Practical Christianity'; in France, Monod's 'Lucille', and in Germany, Arndt's 'True Christianity', have been among the great life-books of their generation; and we may add with confidence to this sacred list the 'Fourfold State' of Boston.

With a quarter of a century after its publication it had found its way, and was eagerly read and pondered, over all the Scottish Lowlands. From St. Abb's Head, in all the Border counties, in the pastoral regions shadowed by the Lammermoors and the Lowthers, to the remotest point in Galloway, it was to be seen, side by side with the Bible and Bunyan's glorious Dream, on the shelf in every peasant's cottage. The shepherd bore it with him, folded in his plaid, up among the silent hills. The ploughman in the valleys refreshed his spirit with it, as with heavenly manna, after his long day of toil. The influence which began with the humbler classes ascended like a fragrance into the mansions of the Lowland laird and the Border chief, and carried with it a new and hallowed joy. The effect was like the reviving breath of spring upon the frost-bound earth. Many a lowly peasant with Boston's 'Fourfold State', familiar through frequent perusal to his memory and heart, became an athlete in the discussion of theological questions, and, like the Border wrestlers in an early age, was rarely worsted in a conflict. One who lived nearer to Boston's age, and was better able to judge, has declared that, over three generations, the 'Fourfold State' had been the instrument of more numerous conversions and more extensive spiritual quickening, in at least one part of our island, than any other human production it was in his power to specify.

It would, however, be a mistake to suppose that even in our own age this remarkable book had at length spent its force, and had become as an old defaced golden coin withdrawn from circulation, or as a sword that had become rusty and unwieldy, and was transferred from the armoury to the museum. In a paper of much ability and interest on 'Religious Thought in Wales', which was not long since read by Principal Edwards at a great meeting of the Presbyterian Alliance in London, it was stated that if you entered the house of a rustic elder or leader of the private societies fifty years ago, you would uniformly find that he had a small and very select library. Among other books you would be sure to lay your hand on translations into Welsh of Boston's 'Fourfold State', Bunyan's 'Pilgrim's Progress', Owen on the 'Person of Christ' and on the 'Mortification of Sin in Believers', and others. It is also true that in our British colonies at the present day, especially where the Scottish element abounds in the population, the 'Fourfold State' continues to be sought after and read; and we have received testimony from natives that it is extensively sold and circulated on the misty coasts of Labrador. It is natural that we should wish to know something of the outer and inner life of an author whom God has honoured for so many generations and in so many lands as the instrument of the highest form of blessing.

It was not only, however, as the author of the 'Fourfold State', and of other books that are afterwards to be named, but as the pastor of Ettrick, that the name of Boston long since obtained a secure and sacred place in the annals of the Church of Christ in Scotland and in the hearts of her people. The assertion is not likely to be challenged that, if Scotland had been searched during the earlier part of the eighteenth century, there was not a minister of Christ within its bounds who, alike in his personal character and in the discharge of his pastoral functions, approached nearer to the apostolic model than did this man of God. It is a fact that, even before he died, men and children had come to pronounce his name with reverence. It had become a synonym for holy living. Away up among these green hills and limpid streams of Ettrick, he rises before our imagination as a man striving daily to lead a saintly life, endeavouring by much thought and prayer to solve for himself difficult theological problems, and doing earnest battle against the profanity, impurity, worldliness, and loose notions and practices in bargain-making which he found to prevail among his parishioners, and to win them to the obedience of Christ. He was such a man as might have sat as a living model to Baxter when he wrote his 'Reformed Pastor'. We would place him as a companion spirit, like-minded and like-gifted, to that 'gentle saint of Nonconformity', as a pious English bishop has recently termed him, Philip Henry of Broad-Oak.

It must be known to many that Boston wrote a 'Memoir' of himself, or, more correctly, kept a diary, which was principally designed for the benefit of his family and 'inner friends', after he had finished his course. It is a large volume, and is invaluable to the biographer both on account of the fulness and accuracy of its information, and because it introduces us to a knowledge of the writer's inward and spiritual life, which, in its degree, would have been impossible except in an autobiography. Next to the 'Confessions of Saint Augustine', with their terrible fidelity of self-revelation, it would be difficult to name any autobiography, in any language, which bears so unmistakably throughout the marks of simplicity and truth. In so far as self-display and self-laudation are concerned, Boston forgets himself even when he is writing of himself. In regard to the incidents of his early life and his early ministry, and to the experiences of his last years, when begun defection in the church drew him forth reluctantly into ecclesiastical conflict, and the spirit of the martyr showed itself in the good confessor, the biographer must derive much of his information from Boston.

But it is from the records of his Ettrick life and ministry that we gather our most precious stores. To the Christian reader there is a sacred and heart-stirring interest in marking that abounding and ardent prayer which was as the air he breathed; in his practice of seeing God, not only in extraordinary providences, but in the common round of daily life; and not less in noticing the severity with which he searched his heart and judged himself as if he felt himself standing in the burning light of divine omniscience, and the sweet tenderness with which he ruled his house, and the holy passion with which his spirit yearned for the salvation of his children. While to the ministers of religion the Ettrick experiences of Boston, as he himself has described them, are full of the most wholesome impulses and suggestive lessons. Alike in his motives and in his methods, as he has enabled us to see him, in his study, in his pulpit, in his pastoral visits, in his meek endurance of opposition, in his perils amid mountain mists and flooded mountain torrents, in his watching for opportunities of doing good, and carving out those opportunities when he did not find them, young ministers when entering on the difficulties and responsibilities of their sacred office may learn the secret of ministerial success, and those who have not succeeded may find out, while it is not yet too late, the secret of their failure.

The more we study that grand Ettrick ministry, the more deep will become our impression that the ideal of a true Christian minister, as traced by Cowper in his well-known lines, and by Paul himself, was in an extraordinary measure realized by this man of

God. In later generations Ettrick has become classic ground. In the poems of Sir Walter Scott and of James Hogg, 'the great minstrel and the shepherd poet', as Wordsworth has happily designated them, every glen and hill and stream has been made sacred to literature, and its name has been wafted to the ends of the earth. But it is to be remembered that two generations before these masters in poetry had struck the chords of their lyre, Ettrick had already become a household word in all the cottages and castles of the Scottish Lowlands, through its association with the name of Boston, who by his writings and his ministry had, in many a parish, turned the wilderness into a fruitful field, and guided many a bewildered wanderer into the kingdom of God.

2

FROM BIRTH TO EARLY MANHOOD – SCHOOLS AND SCHOOLMASTERS

Thomas Boston was born on the 17th day of March 1676, twelve years before the benign Revolution of 1688, which placed William of Orange on the British throne, and reinstated the Presbyterian Church in its emoluments and privileges. His birthplace was Duns, an important town in Berwickshire, situated on a fine plain to the south of Duns Law, which, in spite of broom and furze, still retains the vestiges of its occupation by General Leslie in the stormy times of Cromwell and the Commonwealth.

This neat Border town has been more than usually distinguished as the birthplace of eminent Scotsmen. It claims, not without preponderating evidence in its favour, to have been the native town of John Duns Scotus, some time in the later part of the thirteenth century, who maintained an almost unrivalled reputation for learning, dialectic subtlety, and eloquence over all Europe, until the scholastic theology and philosophy were exploded. It was said of him by one of his contemporaries, that 'he wrote so many books that one man was hardly able to read them, and no one man was able to understand them.' It became the birthplace of Boston in the seventeenth century, and, about a hundred years afterwards, of Dr. Thomas M'Crie, who did so much to enrich the ecclesiastical history of Scotland by his lives of Knox and Melville.

Boston's parents belonged to that humbler middle class who have always formed a large part of the moral salt of Scotland. Reputable among their neighbours, his father, John Boston, was, as his son loved to describe him, an intelligent and pious man, 'having got good of the gospel from his youth'; his mother, Alison Trotter, was 'a woman prudent and virtuous'. Thomas, the subject of our narrative, was the youngest of seven children.

During the interval of twelve years between the birth of Thomas and the enlargement and liberty which came with the Revolution, both parents, who refused to bend to prelatic authority, and preferred peace of conscience to outward ease and the pleasing of men, were made to suffer severely for their Nonconformity. For this offence alone the father was cast into prison. It is the earliest reminiscence of the boy that he was taken into prison with the father to relieve his loneliness. The experience left a deep mark on the child's memory, and he often rejoiced, in his mature years, that he had thus been honoured to have fellowship with his father in his sufferings. One is reminded of something kindred in experience to this in the history of another Nonconformist family. The father of that Isaac Watts who, by his hymns, was destined to make all the churches and all succeeding generations his debtor, was also a Nonconformist, and lay in prison for his Nonconformity at the time when the future hymn-writer was born. The little Isaac was carried from day to day, in his mother's arms, to the prison gate, near to which she would sit for hours on a large stone nursing her infant; for she knew that the innocent sufferer whom she was not allowed to see was soothed and comforted by his knowledge of their presence there.

There is one reminiscence which shows how much the mother was of the same mould and metal as her husband in refusing to obey men in opposition to the demands of conscience, and, at the same time, how fully her woman's heart was in sympathy with him in his sufferings; and she did her utmost to relieve them. On occasion of a second act of disobedience, she made every effort, by her self-straining and industry, to provide the cruel fine which was imposed by the magistrate, with the alternative penalty of imprisonment or the spoiling of his goods. On venturing to ask for some slight abatement on the charge, she was refused with oaths and imprecations of evil. But, according to the Spanish proverb that 'curses like ravens often come home to roost', the malediction speedily returned upon himself in ruin and disgrace. We proceed with the story of the son's life.

At an early age young Boston was sent to school. For three years he was under the care of a 'dame', or schoolmistress, whose manner of teaching was of a very simple and primitive kind, different in many ways from our modern methods. After the tiny pupil had been sufficiently drilled in the alphabet and in the pronouncing of syllables of two or three letters, his next lesson-book, for reading as well as for spelling, was usually the Proverbs of Solomon or the Shorter Catechism, in both of which even poly-syllables were plentiful. There was no graduated scale then of first, and second, and third standards, to make the ascent easy. It was like requiring the young scholar to climb a ladder that wanted some of its steps, and to take an almost desperate bound upward as he might. Nevertheless, the difficulty was in due time overcome. But in the case of little Boston, the 'good-souled' schoolmistress was not content with the usual routine of teaching, for her heart was drawn out to the gentle boy. It was in an upper chamber in his father's house that she kept her school; and, specially in the long winter nights, when the other children were not present, she not only made him read to her aloud, but repeated to him endless Scripture stories, to which the child listened with wondering delight. We are reminded by the scene of Doddridge's gentle mother amplifying, with all a mother's loving simplicity, the incidents of Holy Writ depicted on the blue Dutch tiles which, according to the fashion of the day, lined the chimney corner, The lessons were never forgotten, for nature always paints her earliest pictures on the memory in undying colours.

At eight years of age, or thereabouts, young Boston, having probably risen in his attainments to the level of his kind schoolmistress, and having already shown a marked capacity for instruction, passed into the grammar school of his native town under the mastership of Mr. James Bullerwall, who, in addition to his promoting his further progress in the elementary branches of education, engaged to instruct him in English grammar, in Latin, in which many of the Scottish schoolmasters had been eminent since the days of George Buchanan, and also to qualify him for translating some of the easier parts of the Greek New Testament. From the first, the boy was diligent and dutiful in his attention to his school tasks, profiting above the rest of his own class, by means of whom his progress was the more slow.

It is interesting to notice the estimate which he formed of himself at this period of his school life, and also to obtain a glimpse of the youth as he appears among his schoolmates on the playground. He says, after his own quaint manner: 'By means of my education and natural disposition I was of a sober and harmless deportment, and preserved from the common vices of children in towns. I was at no time what they call a vicious or roguish boy; neither was I so addicted to play as to forget my business, though I was a dexterous player at such games as required art and nimbleness. And toward the latter end of this period, having had frequent occasion to see soldiers exercised, I had a peculiar faculty at mustering and exercising my school-fellows accordingly, by the several words and motions of the exercise of the musket, they being formed into a body under a captain.'

We cannot help thinking, especially when we call to mind a later passage in his autobiography in which he tells us that 'in the natural temper of his spirit he was timorous', that it would have been for his advantage, both in his school life and afterwards, if he had been a good deal more of an athlete than he was. We say this in full remembrance of the protests of the gentle author of the 'Tirocinium'. It is probable that more of the friendly conflicts of the school-ground would have helped to give Boston's natural timidity to the winds. Athletic exercises in the open air and in the midst of fanning breezes not only benefit the body, but the mind through the body, and no good moral education is complete without them. We should endeavour to keep 'the harp of thousand strings' in tune for God. Looking back upon a period of more than sixty years, we can remember excursions of our school in autumn to the hazel-wood behind the hills, the rush in summer, after school hours, to the swimming feats in the bright river not far off, and the bracing winter amusements, secured by holiday, on the bosom of the frozen lake; and we cherish the conviction that the mental and moral, as well as the physical part of our nature, gained by the exercise.

It was not until some time during the closing years of young Boston's attendance at the grammar school that he came under the supreme influence of the religion of Christ. In the case of those whose earliest thoughts have been associated with Bible instruction, who from their childhood have looked on the example of pious parents and breathed the atmosphere of Christian homes, the great change has often come so gradually and imperceptibly that it was impossible for themselves or others to tell the exact moment of the dawning of the new life. Their sense of sin and their apprehension of the Divine love in Christ were so simultaneous that, according to the beautiful figure of Cesar Malan, their spiritual quickening was like the awakening of an infant by its mother's kiss – the moment that it opened its eyes it looked up into the countenance of love. This was not quite the manner of Boston's great change; neither was it in his case associated with those terrible birth-throes into the new life which are associated with the repentance of some, especially when their previous career has been stained with profanity or vice. His conversion in some of its features was different from both of these, and its story is alike interesting and suggestive.

When, in 1687, James II, for purposes of his own, relaxed the restraints on Presbyterian worship, the Rev. Henry Erskine was one of the first to take advantage of the begrudged boon. Originally he had been a Presbyterian minister at Cornhill, on the south of the Tweed, until, under the Act of Uniformity which extinguished so many of the best lights of English Nonconformity, he had been driven from his charge. During the intervening years he had moved from place to place on both sides of the Border, taking eager advantage of opportunities for preaching wherever they could be found, when at length this sudden outburst of liberty, so soon to be enlarged and consolidated by the Revolution, brought him to Whitsome, a little village down in the Merse, about five miles from Duns. He was a man of gentle birth, being related to one of the noble families of Scotland, of much natural eloquence and evangelical fervour, to whom the preaching of Christ was welcome as the air he breathed. To many it may add a peculiar interest to know that he was the father of Ebenezer and Ralph Erskine, who, many years afterwards, were to become the founders of the Scottish Secession Church.

Considerable numbers of the Duns people, who had long been weary of the sapless and Christless preaching to which they had been constrained to listen in their native town, no longer held back by the dread of fine or imprisonment, were gladly willing on every Sabbath morning to travel all the way to Whitsome to attend upon Mr. Erskine's ministry, which was impregnated by gospel truth and glowed with that love which the gospel inspired. It was indeed a time of refreshing. Never did fainting traveller in an Eastern wilderness more welcome the cooling fountain under the shadow of the palm-trees, than did those weekly pilgrims welcome the message of Heaven's love for which they flocked to Whitsome. And John Boston was regularly there with his son Thomas. Our young scholar was among the first whose heart was effectually touched and won to Christ through Mr. Erskine's preaching in that Border village. Particularly, two sermons, the former on the words, 'O generation of vipers, who hath warned you to flee from the wrath to come?' speaking of man's guilt and ruin; and the second on the text, 'Behold the Lamb of God', holding up before his anxious gaze the cross and the Crucified One as the divinely provided means of his deliverance, marked the great turning-point in his spiritual history, and brought him into 'the valley of decision'. 'By these,' he says, 'I judge, God spake to me. However, I know I was touched quickly after the first hearing, wherein I was like one amazed with some new and strange thing. Sure I am, I was in good earnest concerned for a saving interest in Jesus Christ. My soul went out after him, and the place of his feet was glorious in mine eyes.' From that time, every Sabbath morning, as it dawned upon the young convert, seemed to arise with healing on its wings.

Nor were his benefit and enjoyment confined on those days to the Whitsome assemblies. The conversation of his fellow-pilgrims, especially on their way homeward – many of whom were men of much Christian knowledge and ripe religious experience – was found by him to be so edifying and cheering as to make him unconscious of fatigue and weariness by the way. There were 'Greathearts' in that company; and in their fellowship, in which he listened much but said little, he had no need that any one should explain to him what was meant by the 'communion of saints'. And when winter came with its cold and frost, and he was sometimes alone on his journey, and the swollen stream of the Blackadder, without boat or bridge, needed to be waded by him, he never hesitated or turned back; for he knew that the heavenly manna which was in store for him in the Whitsome sanctuary would a hundredfold more than compensate him for all the sacrifice. 'Such things,' he says, 'were then easy, for the benefit of the word which came with power.'

There was another good influence besides those which have just been named, to which he was accustomed to look back in his riper years with delighted remembrance. He and two of his elder schoolmates were in the habit of meeting frequently in a chamber of his father's house for prayer, the reading of Scripture, and spiritual converse, 'whereby,' he tells us, 'we had some advantage both in point of knowledge and tenderness.' It was probably, in some measure, an imitation by the young lads of what they had seen in the practice of their pious parents. In this case the gratified parents would hail the budding life as a fulfilment of the promise to those in mature age who 'feared the Lord, and spake often one to another,' that 'God would pour out his Spirit upon their seed, and his blessing upon their offspring, and they should spring up as among the grass, and as willows by the water-courses.'

But with this glow of affection in religion, we need not be surprised to find that at this period in his early discipleship there was an alloy of weakness and imperfect knowledge which at times disturbed his stability and peace. He records an experience of this kind by which many young Christians, both before and since, have been perplexed and distressed. We describe it in his own words, and with his own reflections: 'Having read of the sealing of the tribes (Rev. 7), Satan wove a snare for me out of it – namely, that the whole number of the elect, or those who were to be saved, was already made up, and therefore there was no room for me. Thereby one may see what easy work Satan, brooding on ignorance, hath to hatch things which may perplex and keep the party from Christ.' He needed some one to teach him that the doctrine of divine election was never meant to be a barrier to scare away the anxious heart from the fountain of life, but to make those who had drunk of its living waters praise and magnify the divine grace that had led them to it, that they might drink and live for ever. He does not tell us how long he was entangled in this snare, and in what way he was at length delivered from it. Perhaps some words spoken by the good pastor at Whitsome may have been as the stretched-out hand that broke 'the subtle fowler's snare'.

Having passed through the usual curriculum of the grammar school in his native town, and probably exhausted the resources of his master, for he tells us that 'before he left the school he saw no Roman author but what he found himself in some capacity to turn into English', the very practical question now arose in the mind of John Boston, What was next to be done with his promising son Thomas? As the good parents, who, like Zacharias and Elisabeth, 'were righteous before God', without any illusion of parental partiality which sometimes sees a genius in a dunce, marked their son's superior and expanding natural gifts, and noted with delight his young and earnest piety, the thought pressed itself on the minds of both that they should give him to the Lord in the Christian ministry; all the more when they learned from their son himself that his own desires had already begun to point tremblingly in the same direction. Such holy ambition for their children has been no uncommon thing even in troublous times in Scotland, and the Scottish Church in all its best periods has received some of its most eminent ministers from lowly cottage homes. But it was wisely required by the Presbyterian Church of Scotland, from the Reformation downwards, that all entrants into the Christian ministry should pass through a course of preparatory study in one of its universities. And the worthy father was not long in discovering, to his own and his son's great disappointment, that the needed expenditure for this end was beyond his means. The bright dream was marred; the *res angustæ domi* blocked the way. The good purpose, however, was not abandoned; but meanwhile, during the two following years, Thomas was employed in a notary's office in his native town, at the end of which time his father's improved circumstances made it possible for him to fulfil his heart's desire.

The favouring tide had come which was to float his son into the midst of all the new scenes and aspirations of a college life. A similar practice had not been unusual among the children of the English Puritans at some point in their advance to the pastoral office, even when there was no barrier of poverty to hold them back – a memorable instance of which we have in the student days of Matthew Henry, whose 'Commentary', so unique in its excellence, has made all succeeding generations his debtor.

Young Boston was made to see that this temporary delay was for his lasting advantage. God took him into *His* school, that he might thus early 'learn to labour and to wait'. Moreover, in the notary's office he acquired habits of order and business which, as will be seen afterwards, proved of great value to him in later life; and when, at length, he entered the university, it was with more matured faculties, which made his benefit from his studies all the greater. When God delays his blessings, it is that they may come at last with a fuller stream and upon a more prepared heart. This was Boston's own devout acknowledgement long afterwards, when, looking back upon this period of his life, he marked the guiding hand of Providence in all. 'Thus,' says he, 'the Lord, in my setting out in the world, dealt with me, obliging me to have recourse to Himself for this thing, to do it for me. He brought me through many difficulties, tried me with various disappointments, at length carried it to the utmost point of hopelessness, seemed to be laying the grave-stone upon it at the time of my mother's death; and yet, after all, he brought it to pass. And this has been the usual method of Providence with me all along in matters of the greatest weight. The wisdom appearing in leading the blind by a way they knew not, shined in the putting off that matter to this time, notwithstanding all endeavours to compass it sooner; for I am perfectly convinced I was abundantly soon put to the college, being then but in the fifteenth year of my age; and the manner of it was kindly ordered, in that I was thereby beholden to none for that my education; and it made way for some things which Providence saw needful for me.'

3

STUDENT, TUTOR AND PROBATIONER

The face of young Boston was now turned with strong desire towards the Christian ministry. Accordingly, in the beginning of the winter of 1691, he proceeded to Edinburgh to enter on a course of study in the Arts classes of its university, which should extend over three annual sessions – this being required by the Scottish Church of all aspirants to the sacred office before entering on the more direct study of theology. Coming from a country town in Berwickshire, in which almost every inhabitant was known to him, into the midst of the noise and bustle of a large city, without friend or acquaintance to acknowledge him, the somewhat timid youth must for a time have felt a depressing sense of loneliness even in the midst of thousands. But he had reached an age when the desire for knowledge in minds like his becomes intense and sometimes omnivorous; and when he saw vast fields of instruction opening before him that stirred him into intellectual activity, this and higher considerations were not long in dispelling the temporary shadows, and making his university pleasant to him, and himself ready to work with a will.

The information he gives us in his autobiography regarding this period of his life is comparatively scanty. He mentions, however, that in addition to further and more advanced training in the Greek and Roman classics, his prescribed subjects of study were 'logics, metaphysics, ethics and general physics'; the last named of which in our days, when new sciences have in the interval sprung into existence, and others have expanded into almost indefinite magnitude, would demand for even one of its departments the whole period of his triennial curriculum. His own report of the manner in which he acquitted himself is condensed into this modest statement, in which he very considerably underrates himself, that he 'always took pains with what was before him, and pleased the regent'. The proficiency which we discover at a later period in his knowledge of the Greek and Latin languages gives testimony not only to his assiduity but to his success.

From what he tells us of his almost incredibly small expenditure during those three years of his curriculum, we are led to conclude that he restricted himself to much too scanty a fare at his solitary meals; not indeed from any fit of juvenile asceticism, but that he might lighten the burden on the little home exchequer at Duns. Indeed he lets out the fact that during his first two years at the university, having 'tabled himself', he did fare but sparingly. But Nature is sure to exact a heavy interest from those who overdraw their account in her coffers. His over-strained economy was most unwise, and he had to pay dear for it, as many an earnest student has done, in a permanently weakened constitution; though his experience showed, as in the case of Baxter and Doddridge, how much mental energy may live and work in a frail physical frame.

There was one exercise by which our student began to relieve the tedium of his long winter nights, and this was in the study and practice of vocal music, in which he took lessons from a qualified teacher. He gives prominence to this in his diary, and tells us that his voice was good, and that he had delight in music. It formed a pleasant alternative after long hours of severe study, and gradually, as he adopted the practice of singing psalms in private, it became the cherished habit of his life. He delighted in it as holy Herbert did in his lute. He was conscious that it not only soothed his oversensitive spirit when at times he seemed to 'see too clearly and to feel too vividly', but that, in his private devotions, it helped his soul to soar more easily upward, like the lark which sings while it soars. Many good men and ministers in those and earlier days had found the same experience. It is well-known that Philip Henry was not content with singing to himself the fragment of a psalm, but that he sought the full advantage of being brought into sympathy with all its changes of thought and emotion by singing it to the end. The practice is not common in our days, though it is understood that it still lives and lingers among the various sections of our Methodist brethren. One thing we know from personal recollection, that in some of those mountain districts of Scotland over which the influence of Boston in his later years had beneficially spread, it was no uncommon thing, in our own early days, for the shepherds tending their flock away up among the silent hills, to awaken their echoes with the 'grave sweet melody of psalms', until the place hemmed in by the mountains seemed like an oratory or a sanctuary of God's building.

Our young scholar's attendance during the three prescribed annual sessions was at length honourably terminated by his receiving, some time in the summer of 1694, what was then termed *Laureation*. This was something more in value than 'a certificate of satisfaction' which it was the custom to give among the English Nonconformists, and approached nearer in its testimony of proficiency to our degree of Master of Arts.

Having thus completed his three years' course of preparatory study in classical literature, philosophy, and science, and received his Laureation, young Boston's next onward step towards the Christian ministry, to which his heart owned a growing attraction, was to devote himself for a corresponding series of years to the systematic study of theology, the teaching of which to his fellow-men, both as a preacher and as an author, was in a few years to become the congenial work of his life, and ultimately to make his name a household word over all Scotland. The kind and seasonable presentation to him of a bursary by his native Presbytery of Duns and Chirnside opened his heart in gratitude, and relieved his ingenuous mind by assuring him that he would not be unduly drawing for help upon home resources. Accordingly, early in the winter of 1695, certified by a loving testimonial from his presbytery, and laden with commendations, he returned to the university to attend upon its theological classes; a great snowstorm, aggravated by intense cold, for a time stopping his way, for deliverance from which he does not fail to record his devout gratitude when he testifies how it had not only impeded his journey, but for a time even endangered his life.

For any knowledge of the Hebrew language which he received at this period, he appears to have been indebted to a Rev. Mr. Rule; but the benefit must have been slight, for the professor is simply named by him without one grateful note of praise. It is different with the professor of 'theology proper', the Rev. Mr. Campbell, from whose prelections and examinations, as well as encouraging looks and words, he owns himself to have derived lasting benefit. It is pleasing to notice in this age of ours, in which veneration is certainly not an outstanding virtue, especially among the young, the ingenuous enthusiasm with which he dilates on the excellences of his professor. He names him again and again as 'the great Mr. George Campbell', and in one place describes him with felicitous appreciation as 'a man of great learning but excessively modest, undervaluing himself, but much valuing the tolerable performances of his students.'

We are led to conclude from other reminiscences of Boston that much of the instruction was conveyed by means of catechisms and text-books in Latin, which were probably good for their generation, but have long since been superseded or forgotten; and the further information that the professor was accustomed to meet with his students in his chamber as well as in his lecture-room, favours the impression that he thus brought himself into contact with each individual mind in his class, winning the student's confidence, learning his wants, discovering his weak points, drawing out his powers, and kindly helping him to grapple with his difficulties – an immense advantage when the character and personality of the man add to the power and influence of the teacher.

But there was an alternative course open to the student. After a period of regular attendance on the theological classes in the university, he was at liberty to withdraw and place himself under the care of one or other of the presbyteries of the church, for theological training and general oversight; one of the ends intended by this being that the student should have an opportunity of self-support by labouring as a schoolmaster in one of the parish schools, or being engaged as a tutor in some family of rank and social position. It was evidently with a good deal of reluctance and regret that our young theologian, who had found so much profit and enjoyment in sitting at the feet of 'the great Mr. George Campbell', succumbed to this alternative, and made choice yield to necessity, for a time, in a beautiful district in Dumfriesshire. There he taught in a parish school but in the midst of uncongenial surroundings unfavourable to religion and even unfriendly to morality, from which his sensitive nature recoiled and sought, though for a time in vain, to be relieved. At length, a more attractive sphere opened to him in his being engaged as tutor in the family of Colonel Bruce of Kennet in Clackmannanshire. He was to find in this chosen home that there were additional schools in which divine Providence became the teacher, and in which aspirants to the sacred office might learn many a useful lesson which could not be so efficiently taught in theological halls and colleges.

Boston's one pupil, a step-son of Colonel Bruce, was a boy of nine years of age, who attended daily on the parish school, and as the principal work of the tutor consisted in the superintendence of the boy in the preparation of his lessons, and in the oversight of his general conduct, especially during the frequent absence of the head of the family on his military duties, there was a considerable margin of time remaining, even when his lenient studies under his presbytery were taken into account, for works of usefulness that might seem to be laid by divine Providence to his hand. A famine which prevailed in the land and was of long continuance, and which of course pressed with unusual severity on the poor, drew the nascent pastor to their homes, in willing ministries of material help supplied from Kennet House, and also in Christian consolation. He gratefully owns that he obtained many of his most precious lessons in Christian experience from those low-roofed cottages.

Though he did not claim to possess the functions of a family chaplain, he charged himself, during the absence of Colonel Bruce, with the conduct of family worship, associating with this religious instruction. Nor was he slow to reprove sin when, on some occasions, it obtruded itself upon his notice. This part of his action was sometimes resisted, and even resented, as passing beyond his province. But his naturally shrinking and timorous nature stood its ground faithfully, and this experience helped to strengthen him where he was naturally weak. We find him gratefully noting this, in some remarkable sentences which we shall quote. At the same time, we are led to conclude from some words in his diary that there were occasions in which his young zeal was not sufficiently tempered by discretion, or marked by that holy wisdom which selects the *mollia tempora fandi*, and aims to do the right thing at the right time and in the best way. The whole passage is, on more than one account, interesting:

'I am convinced that God sent me to Kennet in order to prepare me for the work of the gospel for which he had designed me; for there I learned in some measure what it was to have the charge of souls; and being naturally bashful, timorous, and much subject to the fear of man, I attained, by what I met with there, to some boldness and not regarding the persons of men when out of God's way. There I learned that God will countenance one in the faithful discharge of his duty, though it be not attended with the desired success; and that plain dealing will impress an awe on the party's conscience, though their corruption still rages against him that so deals with them. It was by means of conversation there that I arrived at a degree of public spirit which I had not before; and there I got a lesson of the need of prudent and cautious management and abridging one's self of one's liberty, that the weak be not stumbled and access to edify them be precluded – a lesson I have in my ministry had a very particular and singular occasion for.'

Our student's habits during all this Kennet period were eminently devotional. We are not therefore surprised to learn from his own grateful testimony that, in spite of drawbacks and hindrances before which a feebler piety would have been discouraged, it was, on the whole, a 'thriving time for his soul'. He set aside times for fasting, which did not, however, so much consist in partial abstinence from food as in temporary isolation, in which he gave himself with mingled prayer to self-examination, especially with reference to heart sins – a practice much more common in those days than in our own, but in respect to which we are disposed to accept the saying of Foster, that 'no man will regret on the day of judgment that he had been a most rigid judge of self.' He had also his seasons of prolonged secret devotion, in which 'prayer overflowed its banks like Jordan in the time of harvest.' These were times of great spiritual strengthening and enlargement, as well as of holy joy, upon which he afterwards delighted to look back, as Jacob may be imagined to have remembered his Bethel dreams and visions, and the two privileged disciples their Emmaus walk. All around Kennet, indeed, there were sacred places linked in his memory with devout experiences in which they had seemed to him as the very gate of heaven. Particularly there was one spot which we have visited, in the orchard around Kennet, and which he describes with characteristic minuteness as 'having been under an apple tree with two great branches coming from the root.' 'There,' says he, 'I anointed the pillar and vowed the vow.'

The prescribed years of his theological training were now approaching their end, when it was expected that our earnest student would at once offer himself to one of the presbyteries within whose bounds he had resided for 'trials and examinations', with a view to his becoming a licentiate or probationer of the Scottish Church, and eligible to the pastoral office in one of its parishes. Good men in those districts, who had learned to appreciate his blossoming gifts and ardent piety, vied with each other in seeking to induce him to apply for license within their bounds. But growing diffidence, arising from a deepened sense of the responsibilities of the pastoral office, made him hesitate for a time about taking the decided step. At length, a visit to Duns on another matter bringing him under the old home influences, his scruples vanished, and he consented to be proposed for license by his native presbytery. An elaborate course of examinations, associated with written exercises in theology, 'dragged its slow length along' through several months, and ended in a unanimous record of approval and resolution to enrol his name on the list of probationers. With mingled feelings of humility and gratitude, the young licentiate now stood within sight of the sacred office which was to him not the object of a mere human ambition, but of a holy passion to serve the best of Masters in the best of causes.

Our probationer's superior preaching gifts were readily acknowledged and appreciated, especially by his more serious and earnest hearers who had had some experience of the power of Christian truth in their own hearts. It is evident, however, that, in the earlier months of his novitiate, his sermons consisted too exclusively in denunciations of sin and threatenings of divine wrath and retribution. It might have been said of him in measure, as Cotton Mather had long before said of the great missionary Elliot, that 'his pulpit was a Mount Sinai, and his words were thunderbolts.' No doubt this was necessary in its own place and degree. The ploughsnare of the law must turn up the furrows for receiving the good seed of the gospel; but the ploughsnare is impotent alone. He had hoped thereby, to quote his own words, 'to set fire to the devil's nest.' But 'old Adam proved too strong for young Melancthon.' A kind hint from a minister of long experience helped the young and intrepid minister to see his mistake. 'If you were entered,' said he, 'on preaching Christ, you would find it very pleasant.' The immediate effect of this word spoken with a wise love was to make him so far modify his strain of preaching, and to season and vitalize all his discourses with the gospel of Heaven's love. From that day no one had cause to complain to him, 'Sir, we would see Jesus.' The change was followed by a life-long gratitude to his fatherly mentor. 'I have often,' said he, 'remembered that word of Mr. Dysart as the first hint given me by the good hand of my God towards the doctrine of the gospel.'

It was natural to anticipate that, in the case of so impressive and attractive a preacher, with so much glowing earnestness of spirit, he would not have needed to wait long for a settlement. Perhaps Boston himself, without any undue self-appreciation, may have shared in this expectation, all the more that there were many vacant parishes longing and looking out for one who should break among them the bread of life; but, in fact, his probation extended over the somewhat protracted and dreary period of two years and three months. The explanation of this lays open some not very pleasing glimpses into the ecclesiastical condition of the times. There were dark shadows and portents upon a picture which revealed many things that were bright and promising. For one thing, though the right of election to the pastoral office in the Scottish Church was nominally in the free call of the people, it was practically to a great extent in the hands of the principal heritor or landed proprietor in the parish, whose veto, though not formally given, was in many instances potent enough to hinder a settlement; and Boston's sense of the sacredness which belonged to the call or free choice of a Christian congregation, as well as his tenderness of conscience, held him sensitively back from any approaches, by way of solicitation or otherwise, to those who, to use his own words, 'had the stroke in such matters.'

Then one of the greatest blunders and most mischievous compromises which helped to vitiate the Revolution Settlement which re-established the Presbyterian Church and restored to her her former immunities, was the allowing as many of the Episcopal incumbents as were willing to accept the Presbyterian polity and form of worship, to continue in their charges, and retain their emoluments. Bishop Burnet declared, in terms which one would like to believe were somewhat over-coloured, that these conformists 'were ignorant to a reproach, many of them openly vicious, and the worst preachers he ever heard.' By a natural instinct, these men with their easy pliancy were almost certain to use their influence and secret manoeuvring and management against such a man as Boston, whose life and character were a standing rebuke and condemnation of theirs. In seven different parishes where the popular voice, if left to its own free and unbiassed choice, would have fallen upon our young evangelist with his expanding gifts and ardent zeal, these hostile forces dashed the cup from his lips. It was impossible that he should not deeply feel these repeated disappointments, though he knew that he owed them in part to his determination, at whatever loss and hazard, not to walk into the sacred office over the body of a wounded conscience.

In the midst of this long succession of hopes deferred, of

expectations which blossomed only to be blighted, it is pleasant to note that his spirit was sustained by the testimonies he received, wherever pulpits were thrown open to him, of the highest forms of blessing which multitudes had derived from his ministry of the Word. Everywhere, as in the fresh bloom of our religion in the preaching of the apostles, 'the Lord gave testimony unto the word of his grace.' It was a frequent experience to be told by some who came to him with streaming eyes that his words had been to them the seeds of a new and heavenly life; while others would be found waiting at the church gates to tell him, with mingled wonder and gratitude, how, while unknown to him, he had seemed by his searching representations to have been reading their history and their hearts. Even ripe and aged saints were not slow to express their astonishment how one so young could reflect in his teaching their deepest and most hidden experiences as 'face answereth to face in a glass.' Could there be any more distinct sealing of the Holy Spirit upon his ministry than this? Thus he interpreted the providence, and 'thanked God, and took courage.'

There is one fact recorded in his experience at this period which is not without its suggestiveness. There were occasions in which he preached under much mental depression and restraint, and these he was sometimes tempted to regard as tokens of divine displeasure and desertion, which, for the time, might leave his ministry unblessed. Probably these alternations of light and shadow in the same day, or even in the same hour, sometimes had their explanation in physical weakness or ill health, as seen and judged by him who 'knoweth our frame, and remembereth that we are dust.' One thing is certain, that some of those very occasions on which there was an absence of happy frames and eloquent speech were signally blest. There was a rich harvest of the sea when the man-fisher seemed to be dragging out from the deep an empty net.

We notice in this trying period of his life the same abounding in prayer, and severe heart-searching and striving against heart sins, which no eye could see but God's, as we remarked in his student life. Again and again we meet with such exclamations as, 'Oh, how my heart hates my heart!' Even some of his dreams wounded his moral sensibility, and he could have prayed with good Bishop Ken,

> 'When in the night I sleepless lie,
> My soul with heavenly thoughts supply;
> Let no ill dreams disturb my rest,
> No powers of darkness me molest.'

We shall introduce another fact in his own words which exemplifies the same habit of unsparing self-scrutiny in connection with somewhat novel conditions. We must imagine our young probationer to have been listening to the preaching of a rival candidate, Mr. J. G., for a vacant charge. Mark how he schools his heart against prejudice, and into just and even generous appreciation:

'On the Saturday's afternoon, there comes a letter to my hand, desiring me to give the one-half of the day to Mr. J. G., whom those that were against me had an eye upon. The letter I received contentedly, granted the desire of it, and blessed the Lord for it. In these circumstances, seeing what hazard I was in from an evil prejudice, I committed my heart to the Lord that I might be helped to carry evenly. I cried to the Lord for it, and got that word, 'My grace shall be sufficient for thee.' On Sabbath morning, I found in myself a great desire to love Christ and to be concerned solely for his glory; and prayed to that effect not without some success. He (Mr. J. G.) got the forenoon, for so it was desired by them. I was helped to join in prayer, was much edified both by his lecture and sermon, yet, in the time, I was thrice assaulted with the temptation I feared; but looking up to the Lord, got it repulsed in some measure, and found my soul desirous that people should get good, soul-good, of what was very seriously, pathetically, and judiciously said to us by the godly young man. Betwixt sermons I got a sight of my own emptiness, and then prayed and preached in the afternoon with much help from the Lord. Yet for all that, I wanted not some levity of spirit, which poison my heart sucked out of that sweet flower.'

On the whole much genuine gold was revealed by that crucible of fire.

Two years of this probationary life had now come and gone, and the prospect of settlement in a parochial charge seemed as remote as ever. Mr. Boston began to question with himself whether the many tokens of divine blessing upon his somewhat wandering ministry were not to be regarded by him as providential signs that his mission was rather to be that of an evangelist itinerating and preaching from place to place, than that of a settled pastor. But such an arrangement did not seem practicable. To quote his own words, 'he had now reached the full sea-mark of his perplexing circumstances. He felt like one standing in the dark, and not knowing what his next step should be.' We notice in his diary at this period a growing heavenliness of spirit and a more unqualified self-surrender or willingness to follow whithersoever God might lead, blaming himself with more severity than others generally would have done for the occasional risings of itching desires after a settlement. Texts of Scripture like the following were as ointment poured forth: 'The meek will he guide in judgment, and the meek will he teach his way' – 'He hath determined the times before appointed, and the bounds of their habitation.' And we find these words in his diary: 'My soul desires to lay itself down at his feet. Let him do with me as he will. I am his own.'

And now had come 'the time for God to work.' In the small parish of Simprin, down in the Merse, about five miles towards the east of Duns, 'least among the thousands of Judah', God had provided for him a sphere in which he should find welcome rest in the congenial work of a minister of Christ. The rustic people were unanimous in their choice of him for their pastor, and for the first time in his experience there was no spectral lay-patron to neutralize the people's action and to stop the way. The principal heritor cordially joined with the simple people in their call, and with no vitiating elements to make his course of duty uncertain, he heard the voice of God in the voice of the people, and obeyed it. We can imagine devout ministers in some of the surrounding parishes to have wondered much that a man of such rare gifts and capabilities should have been placed by the manifest leadings of Providence in so narrow a sphere. As for Mr. Boston himself, if such a question as this ever for a moment cast its shadow over his mind, he thought of his responsibility for the care of souls, 'watching for them as those who know that they must give an account,' and was satisfied. Moreover, we find him saying in one of his mental soliloquies, 'I know not what honourable use the Lord may have for me there.' But could those kindly onlookers whom we have imagined have been permitted to look on the whole of that plan of God of which every good man's life is the development, their wonder would have been turned into praise. Simprin was the chosen place in which, through strangely varied incidents in which God was pleased to work, Boston should receive great enlargement in his knowledge of divine things, which should not only be of large and lasting benefit to himself and his ministry, but should favourably influence the religious thought and teaching of Scotland for generations to come. Moreover, within seven busy years he was, by his earnest preaching not taught in the schools of human rhetoric, but kindled and sustained by fire from off the altar of God, by his pastoral oversight and all-pervading prayer, to transform his parish, putting a new look upon everything, and to 'cause the desert to blossom as the rose.' Surely this more than solved the mystery. We find him writing many a year afterwards in grateful and adoring retrospect, 'I will ever remember Simprin as a field which the Lord blessed.'

'When obstacles and trials seem
Like prison walls to be,
I do the little I can do,
And leave the rest to Thee.

Ill that He blesseth is our good,
And unblest good is ill;
And all is right that seem most wrong,
If it be His sweet will.'

We shall be forgiven if, in closing this chapter, we mention the fact that, in the latter part of his course as a probationer, Mr. Boston composed a small treatise, which evidently grew out of passing experiences, and which, in its devout thinking and practical sagacity, would have been worthy of a minister of twice his age. The little book was not published at the time, but only appeared after a long interval. We shall enrich our chapter by quoting a few sentences. It was entitled 'A Soliloquy on the Art of Man-fishing'; and it was founded on those words of Jesus to Simon and Andrew when, standing by the seaside, he called them away from their employment as fishermen, in order that they might be trained and qualified by him for becoming the ministers and apostles of his religion, and thus coming forth at length as 'fishers of men'. The young author explains that when Jesus thus said to those sincere and simple men, 'Follow me,' his language meant a great deal more than, 'Leave your nets and boats and come after me, and learn to be the preachers of my word'; but, in addition, that if they would do good to souls, and gain them to him by their ministry, then they were to imitate him 'in their character and preaching, to make him their pattern, to write after his copy, as a fit means for the gaining of souls.'

4

HIS MINISTRY IN SIMPRIN

Mr. Boston was ordained at Simprin on 21st September 1699. He had now reached the object of his holy ambition, and was ready to say of his church and parish, 'This is my rest, here will I dwell. I found my heart well content with my lot, and the sense of God's calling me to that work with the promise of his presence. Oh, it satisfies my soul, and my very heart blesseth him for it. For really it is the doing of the Lord, and wondrous in my eyes.'

The text from which he preached on the first Sabbath after his ordination struck the loud and solemn keynote of his whole ministry: 'For they watch for souls as they that must give an account.' The solemn thought of the care of souls which, as a preacher, he must feed with the manna of heavenly truth, and as a pastor he must tend and guide in the way of life, with the foresight of that day of reckoning in which he must give an account of his stewardship, haunted him like an angel's presence, and made him well content with the obscurity of his position, the rustic manners of his people, and the smallness of his charge. A mere hireling, whose earthborn ambition never rose above a comfortable manse, a good stipend, and a respectable social position, would have turned away from poor Simprin with disappointment or disdain, because he was an hireling; all the more that both church and manse were dilapidated and going fast to ruin, and the people had been described as generally ignorant and coldly indifferent. But our young minister judged of the matter by another standard. There was even a peculiar fascination to his consecrated spirit in his being called to 'break up the fallow ground', and to give his days and nights to the winning of souls. Was not this the part of the Lord's vineyard to which God had appointed him? And woe was unto him if he turned a deaf ear to the divine voice which said to him, 'Go and work there.'

We find Mr. Doddridge, the author of 'The Rise and Progress of Religion in the Soul,' in the same spirit, though more in a vein of contented pleasantry, writing to a friend who had condoled with him in a letter on his being buried alive in the obscure country village of Kibworth. He admits that his rustic flock consisted mainly of graziers and their dependants. 'I have not,' he adds, 'so much as a tea-table in my whole diocese, although eight miles in extent, and but one hoop petticoat within the whole circuit. I am now with a plain, honest, serious people. I heartily love them myself, and I meet with genuine, undissembled affection on their side. Instead of lamenting it as my misfortune, you should congratulate me upon it as my happiness that I am confined to an obscure village, seeing that it gives me so many advantages to the most important purposes of devotion and philosophy, and I hope I may add of usefulness too.'

Eight days after his ordination, Mr. Boston renewed his dedication of himself to God, and subscribed anew his solemn covenant in the following characteristic document, which long afterwards was found among his papers:

'I, Mr. Thomas Boston, preacher of the gospel of Christ, being by nature an apostate from God, an enemy to the great Jehovah, and so an heir of hell and wrath, in myself utterly lost and undone, because of my original and actual sins, and misery thereby; and being, in some measure, made sensible of this my lost and undone state, and sensible of my need, my absolute need, of a Saviour, without whom I must perish eternally; and believing that Jesus Christ, the eternal Son of the eternal God, is not only able to save me (though most vile and ugly, and one who has given him many repulses), both from my sins and from the load of wrath due to me for them, upon condition that I believe, come to him for salvation, and cordially receive him in all his offices, consenting to the terms of the covenant: therefore, as I have, at several opportunities before, given an express and solemn consent to the terms of the covenant, and have entered into a personal covenant with Christ, so now, being called to undertake the great and mighty work of the ministry of the gospel for which I am altogether insufficient, I do by this declare that I stand to and own all my former engagements, whether sacramental or any other whatsoever: and now again do renew my covenant with God; and hereby, at this present time, do solemnly covenant and engage to be the Lord's, and make a solemn resignation and upgiving of myself, my soul, body, spiritual and temporal concerns, unto the Lord Jesus Christ, without any reservation whatsoever; and do hereby give my voluntary consent to the terms of the covenant laid down in the Holy Scriptures, the word of truth; and with my heart and soul I take and receive Christ in all his offices, as my Prophet, to teach me, resolving and engaging in his strength to follow, that is, to endeavour to follow, his instructions: I take him as my Priest, to be saved by his death and merits alone; and renouncing my own righteousness as filthy rags and menstruous cloths, I am content to be clothed with his righteousness alone, and live entirely upon free grace: likewise I take him for my Advocate and Intercessor with the Father: and, finally, I take him as my King, to reign in me and to rule over me, renouncing all other lords, whether sin or self, and in particular my predominant idol; and in the strength of the Lord do resolve and hereby engage to cleave to Christ as my sovereign Lord and King, in death and in life, in prosperity and in adversity, even for ever, and to strive and wrestle in his strength against all known sin; protesting that whatever sin may be lying hid in my heart out of my view, I disown it and abhor it, and shall, in the Lord's strength, endeavour the mortification of it when the Lord shall be pleased to let me see it. And this solemn covenant I make as in the presence of the ever-living, heart-searching God, and subscribe it with my hand, in my chamber at Dunse, about one o'clock in the afternoon, the fourteenth day of August, one thousand six hundred and ninety-nine years. T. Boston.'

Pastoral work

The young minister lost no time in entering on his sacred work. 'The King's business required haste.' It was true that the half-ruined and uninhabitable condition of his manse made it necessary that he should reside for a time in Duns, which was about six miles distant, and this both consumed much of his time and impeded his labours. But still he would do what he could, and while his work was unpleasantly diminished, this was no reason why it should stand still.

It was reasonable that one of his earliest measures should be the visitation of every household in his parish, not only that he might endeavour to win the confidence of his people in his good intentions, and that they might be convinced of his earnestness of purpose, but that he might ascertain for himself the amount of their Christian knowledge and their general moral and religious condition. The diagnoses was disappointing and saddening. The whole truth had not been told him. Their ignorance was such that they needed to be instructed in the simplest elements of divine truth, and their indifference to everything spiritual and heavenly was in proportion to their ignorance. Their thoughts were bounded by the ploughing of their fields, the sowing of their seeds, and the gathering in of their crops, in the circle of the seasons. Two facts revealed much. In all that parish, with its seventy 'examinable' persons, he could find only one house in which there was the observance of family worship. And such was the prevailing spiritual death, or languor that was on the verge of death, that the Lord's Supper had not once been observed in the parish for several years. We can imagine the devoted young pastor, as he realized the cheerless picture, again and again putting to himself the question, 'Can these dry bones live?' and yet, in another moment of kindling hope, prostrating himself in the solitude of his little prophet's chamber, and sending up the cry to heaven, 'Come from the four winds, thou Spirit of the Lord, and breathe upon these slain, that they may live.' This was the condition in which he found Simprin. We are now to see what it became under his ministry, and by what means, in the following seven years.

He proceeded to 'build up the waste places', and to set in order the various agencies of an earnest ministry. The forenoon and afternoon Sabbath services, which had long been irregularly and fitfully observed, were instituted anew; the smallness of the parish having this advantage, that it made attendance easy even for the most remote parishioner. Already alive to the fact that such a people needed, in the first instance, a ministry of conviction and alarm, such as that of Elliot in olden times,[1] or that of John the Baptist on the banks of the Jordan among the self-satisfied and hardened Pharisees, his earliest discourses, with their glowing personal applications to his somewhat astonished hearers, were principally on man's depravity and guilt; as if he had already in his mind the germ of that 'Fourfold State' which, in another age, was to exercise so powerful and beneficent an influence upon the religious thought and the spiritual life of Scotland.

Simultaneously with this, he commenced the lifelong practice of pastoral visitation from house to house, its predominant services consisting in religious exhortation and prayer. To this he continued to attach an importance only second to his pulpit ministrations, not merely because of its direct influence, but because it brought him into direct contact with individual minds, and made him acquainted with the history and condition of the individual families, while it helped him the better to select topics seasonable for pulpit instruction, and to adapt them to their business and bosoms. One is apt to think that his gift of music must often have been brought into service in the singing of psalms, in the winding up of those edifying family gatherings. And when, in the depth of winter, with his church restored and his manse renovated and made inhabitable, he was able at length to give his whole strength and time to his sacred work, he proceeded to institute a Sabbath-evening service for his people, in order to their more familiar and systematic instruction in the elementary truths of the Christian

---

1. *Editor's note*: The author may be referring to John Elliot (1604–90), a missionary to the Red Indians during the Puritan period, whose dedicated life was a challenge to many ministers and missionaries of subsequent centuries.

faith, in which he found them most grievously ill-informed; uniting with this the catechetical examination of his hearers, one by one, in the lessons which they had heard.

We find in his autobiography a summary statement of his instructions in one of those Sabbath-evening exercises, on the subject of 'divine providence', which we may take as a specimen. In common with the Nonconformists of England at the same period, he seems to have taken the Shorter Catechism as his text-book, while leaving himself free for individual freedom of treatment. 'The evening service concerning the providence of God was sweet to me; and in converse after it, it was a pleasure to think and speak of the saint's grounds of encouragement for that head – under trouble, particularly, how it is their God that guides the world, and nothing do they meet with but what comes through their Lord's fingers; how he weighs their troubles to the least grain, that no more falls to their share than they need; and how they have a covenant right to chastisements, to the Lord's dealing with them as with sons, to be rightly educated, not as servants whom the master will not strike but send away at the term.'

We are struck with the evidence which the whole of our young minister's plan and action at this period affords us of the earnest anxiety with which he thought for his people in all his arrangements. The practice of questioning his hearers on those Sabbath evenings, immediately after his familiar conversational lessons, enabled him at once to see how far he had succeeded in making himself understood, and gave him an opportunity of reiterating his instructions, and of further explanation where he saw it to be needed. He was unwilling to move beyond their pace. Another fact reveals his conscientiousness and zeal in these instructions. He tells us that he endeavoured to enlist and retain their attention and interest by the free use of similitudes drawn from the natural world, enlisting their imaginations by those natural pictures. But in his first endeavours, he was disappointed, and mortified to find that he had only half succeeded. His catechizings brought to light the fact that while they remembered the similitudes, they failed to retain the divine truths of which they were meant to be the vehicle; kept hold of the earthly, but let drop the heavenly; relished the shell, but not the kernel. 'The natural man receiveth not the things of the Spirit of God.'

But this monotony of unfruitfulness was not long to continue. Before spring was ended, there began to appear signs not only of awakening inquiry but of spiritual quickening, like the music of the early songbirds, which not only tells us that winter is past, but is hailed as a prophecy of summer. The heart of the young pastor was gladdened by these few but welcome experiences. He thought that he saw in them the sealing of the Holy Spirit upon his labours, and that their voice to him was, 'Be of good cheer'; and they sent him to his closet with songs of thanksgiving, so that he could already write in his diary: 'With joy I saw myself in Simprin as in my nest, and under the covert of Christ's wings.'

Marriage
But when midsummer came, there occurred an event which, next to his conversion and ordination to the Christian ministry, exercised the most important and beneficent influence upon all his future life. Early in his probationer life, he had formed an acquaintance with a lady of good family in Clackmannanshire, which had speedily ripened into a tender affection. He informs us, indeed, that on the first day on which he looked on her his heart had been drawn out to her with a preference which increased with interaction, while it was fully reciprocated by the object of his choice. And what helped much to strengthen his love, while it introduced into it a new and sacred element, was the living religious sympathy which existed between them, so that Boston beheld in his Catherine Brown not only a sweetheart but a sister in Christ. He tells us, in his own characteristic manner, that from the first 'he discerned in her the sparkles of grace'. Had this divine quality been wanting, or its existence even dubious, it was certain that he would never have told his love. But there was no cause even for uncertainty; and the consequence was that the honourable attachment which, in his own words, 'needed rather to be bounded than strengthened', soon ripened into mutual devotement and

51

betrothal, to be consummated in honourable wedlock when Providence should make their way plain, and should be ready to arise and bless the banns.

Probably neither of them anticipated that a period of nearly three years would intervene before marriage would be made practicable through Mr. Boston's settlement in a pastoral charge. And there must have been an occasional sinking of the heart on the part of both when the cup of ecclesiastical preferment, as it rose to his lips, was again and again dashed away. But during all that wearisome interval of hope deferred, the betrothed maiden looked on with quiet and trustful patience, giving no sign of murmuring or disappointment, and did much to encourage Boston in waiting God's time, which would be seen and owned by them to be the best when it came. It was with reference to this, as well as to later periods, that we find him making this grateful record: 'I was made often to bless the Lord that ever I was made acquainted with her.'

But when Boston became minister of the church and parish of Simprin, every barrier to marriage was taken out of the way, and about ten months afterwards the two attached friends, whose hearts had for years been one, joined hands in holy wedlock, and pledged themselves to each other by sacred bonds which nothing but death could sever. The solemn rite, which had been preceded by much heart-searching and prayer, and was engaged in with a deep and chastened joy, took place at Culross, on the banks of the Forth, on July 17, 1700, and was conducted by the Rev. Mr. Mair, who was Boston's friend, and minister of the parish. 'The action,' says Mr. Boston, 'was gone about most sweetly by Mr. Mair. The Lord directed him to most seasonable and pertinent exhortations, and they came with power and life. Of a truth God owned it, and it was sweet both to him and to us.' A few days afterwards, when the grateful husband led his bride into the humble manse of Simprin, he felt that he had indeed received a gift from the Lord. The words of Luther when writing of his wife Catherine Bora would not have been unsuitable to Boston when speaking of his wife Catherine Brown: 'The greatest gift of God is an amiable and pious spouse who fears God, loves his house, and with whom one can live in perfect peace.' It was a union which stood the tests of time and trial.

Thirty years after his marriage, we find Mr. Boston bearing his testimony to this in words which have often been admired since, and in whose holy beauty, tenderness, and gushing thankfulness he rises above himself: 'Thus was I, by all-wise Providence, yoked with my wife, with whom I have now, by the mercy of God (1730), lived thirty years complete; a woman of great worth, whom I therefore passionately loved and inwardly honoured; a stately, beautiful, and comely personage, truly pious, and fearing the Lord; of an evenly temper, patient in our common tribulations and under her personal distresses; a woman of bright natural parts and an uncommon stock of prudence; of a quick and lively apprehension in things she applied herself to; of great presence of mind in surprising incidents; sagacious and acute in discerning the qualities of persons, and therefore not easily imposed upon; modest and grave in her deportment, but naturally cheerful; wise and affable in conversation, having a good faculty at speaking and expressing herself with assurance; endowed with a singular dexterity in dictating of letters; being a pattern of frugality and wise management of household affairs, therefore entirely committed to her; well fitted for and careful of the virtuous education of her children; remarkably useful to the country-side, both in the Merse and in the Forest, through skill in physic and surgery, which, in many instances, a peculiar blessing appeared to be commanded upon from heaven; and, finally, a crown to me in my public station and appearances. During the time we have lived together hitherto, we have passed through a sea of trouble as not seeing the shore but afar off. I have sometimes been likely to be removed: she having had little continued health except the first six weeks, her death hath sometimes stared us in the face, and hundreds of arrows have pierced my heart on that score; and sometimes I have gone with a trembling heart to the pulpit, laying my account with being called out of it to see her expire. And now for the third part of the time we have lived together – namely, ten years complete – she has been under a particular racking distress, and for several of these years fixed to her bed; in the which furnace the grace of God in her hath been brightened, her parts continued to a wonder, and her beauty, which formerly was wont upon her recoveries to leave no vestige of the illness she had been under, doth as yet, now and then, show some vestiges of itself.'

It was probably not long after his marriage that the earnest minister, ever on the outlook for new opportunities of benefiting his people, threw open his house to any who might be willing to attend on his morning family worship. Nor is it difficult to believe that his young wife, who was ready to be his helpmate in his ministry as well as in the common details of home life, would sympathize with him in this arrangement, and, casting aside all thoughts of domestic inconvenience, would give cordial welcome to all that came. The project was successful. Many of his parishioners came regularly to the service. Mr. Boston mingled with the devotional exercises a brief exposition of Scripture, for which he never failed to prepare himself by previous study; and the interested worshippers returned to their home care, or their out-of-door industry, toned for the day.

Trials

But his sky was not to be long without clouds. The first year of his Simprin pastorate was scarcely ended, when he was called to mourn over the death of his father, in his seventieth year. The stroke was not unexpected, but, as he tells us in his diary, 'it went to the quick with him.' 'It was a heavy death to me, the shock of which I had much ado to stand.' There were filial ties and sacred memories of peculiar strength and tenderness which bound him to his father. He remembered how, when a boy, he had borne him company night and day when he was suffering imprisonment for conscience' sake. He could not forget the sacrifices which he had made for a series of years, out of his straitened means, in order to obtain for him such a university education as was required of candidates for the Christian ministry. And ever since, the hoary head had been found in the way of righteousness. There must have been grateful joy, mingled with natural sorrow, when the bereaved son could write thus of his father: 'He was one who, in the worst times, retained his integrity beyond many; and in view of death gave comfortable evidences of eternal life to be obtained through the Lord Jesus Christ.'

A few weeks after the father's death, another event happened in the family history, in which joy and sorrow were strangely mingled. On the 24th May 1701, Mrs. Boston gave birth to her first child, Catherine, 'having,' says the devout father, 'at the holy and just pleasure of the sovereign Former of all things, a double harelip, whereby she was rendered incapable of sucking.' On the way to the chambers he was met by the nurse, who intimated to him the case of the child, 'with which,' says he, 'my heart was struck like a bird shot and falling from a tree. Howbeit,' he adds, 'I bore it gravely, and my afflicted wife carried the trial very Christianly, and wisely after her manner.' It was a weakly child, requiring to be watched night and day through all the months of summer; but when autumn came, the little one began to revive.

Money affairs requiring that Mr. Boston and his wife should visit her former home in Clackmannanshire, they proceeded thither in the beginning of harvest. On their return home after a brief stay, made shorter on account of Mrs. Boston's imperfect health, they rested for a night in her sister's house at Torryburn, Fifeshire. There, in the morning before rising from bed, she had a remarkable dream. She dreamed that she saw her child perfect in form, 'the natural defect being made up, and extraordinarily beautiful.' This making an impression on their minds to which they could not be indifferent, they hastened their way homeward. On arriving at Black's Mill, about nine miles from Simprin, they were met by friends, when their hearts were pierced with the information that their little infant was both dead and buried. 'After which,' says Mr. Boston, 'we came home in great heaviness, and found that that very day and hour of the day, as near as could be judged, when my wife had the dream aforesaid, the child had died.' They could not help connecting the death with the dream which had been sent to them beforehand 'with healing on its wings.'

Early pastoral experiences

It may be interesting to some ministers of Christ in our own days to be told of some of our young pastor's early ministerial experiences – those 'lessons in black print,' as Foster calls them. They may even suggest valuable hints both for encouragement and warning. In the earlier years of his Simprin life, he had frequent difficulty in fixing on a text for the following Sabbath. Sometimes, even more time was consumed in finding a text that suited his present state of mind, than was usually occupied in the composition of a sermon. There was something more than perplexity and worry in this, when, as occasionally happened, the week was already far advanced, and in his growing anxiety he seemed to hear the sound of the Sabbath bell summoning him to his sacred work. This was even beyond the experience of John Newton, the good pastor of Olney, who was seldom helped to more than one text in the week, and who compared himself to a servant to whom a key had been given that only opened one drawer at a time, but never had committed to him a bunch of keys which opened all the drawers.

But in his later years at Simprin, it was Mr. Boston's custom to select large paragraphs of Scripture, which, in their succession of verses, supplied texts for many sermons – a practice which carried with it the great advantage of enabling him, sometimes consciously and sometimes unconsciously, to gather material from his reading and observation, not only for the wants of the present week, but for those of many weeks to come. We find him, for instance, lingering over the few verses of the epistle to the Church of Laodicea from January to the end of May, and apparently loath to leave the passage even then, with the feeling that the golden mine had not yet been made to yield up all its riches. One statement which he makes is specially valuable and suggestive, that his afflictions not unfrequently found his texts for him, and that those sermons were the most profitable to others which had taken their shape and colouring from his personal and family history, and had been suggested by the events of his own life.

A valuable lesson may also be gleaned by some from another

experience in his early ministry. It had been his practice, at first, to delay his preparations for his pulpit to the last days of the week, the consequence of which too often was that when Saturday came much of his sermon yet remained to be written. It was not long ere he began to find the inconvenience and evil of this delay, and to resolve that the writing of his discourses for the Sabbath should be over, at the latest, on the Friday evenings. In more than one respect he found the advantage of this wise change. The intervening rest of Saturday secured for him a greater reserve of strength and freshness for his Sabbath ministrations. It may even have preserved him at times from mistaking mental and physical depression for divine desertion. It saved him also from the fretting and worry which were certain to come out of undue haste or inconvenient interruptions, while it gave him time to preach the sermon to his own heart before he preached it to his people. Much is revealed regarding his frequent state of mind on closing the writing of one of his sermons: 'Oh that it were written in my heart as it is in my book.'

It must have been a painful surprise to a minister of such lofty aims and gentle charity as Mr. Boston, to have been told by certain of his hearers that he was suspected of indulging in 'personalities' in his preaching, and that they even believed that, in some things which he had recently spoken, he had been aiming at them. It is superfluous to say that few things can be more unworthy of a minister of Christ, or a more shameful degrading of his sacred office, than when he uses his pulpit to gratify a secret vindictiveness or spite. But such suspicions are commonly groundless, and are to be accounted for by an overweening self-importance on the part of some of his hearers, or by an uneasy conscience in others, which smarts under faithful preaching when it unveils to the man some secret besetting sin, or purpose of evil. Indeed it is a poor sign of a minister's discriminating skill and fidelity in his pulpit when his preaching does not at times make individuals among his hearers uneasy almost to resentment, and his 'drowsy tinklings only lull his flock to sleep.' 'I should suspect his preaching had no salt in it,' says the wise and witty Thomas Fuller, 'if no galled jade did wince. But still it does not follow that the archer aimed because the arrow hit.'

Some of our readers will be interested by another phase in Mr. Boston's early Simprin experiences. We find him mourning again and again over the fewness of his books, and especially of commentaries on the Word of God. He even described himself in one place as having been wounded in his feelings, 'touched to the quick', by observing the smile which passed over the countenance of a brother minister from a neighbouring parish, when he showed him his little book-press with its scantily supplied shelves. Among the cherished few, he tells us, were Zanchy's works, and Luther on the Galatians, 'which he was much taken with'; and Providence also laid to his hand Beza's 'Confession of Faith'. Circulating libraries, and books posts, and other expedients with which the modern country parson is gratefully familiar, were unknown in those days, and there is no evidence that the weekly carrier's cart from the great city regularly touched at Simprin. Only once in the year did our pastor's straitened means admit of his bringing home a carefully selected book parcel, not very portly, to add to his little stores. He came, however, ere long to see that there were compensating advantages even in this. For he had time to read and digest the supplies of one year before the next greedily-waited-for annual parcel of books arrived. The reproach could not have been flung at him that it was more easy to furnish our library than our understanding. And even by his lack of commentaries, he was thrown back the more upon his own mental resources, and closed up to independent thought; while he early began to register in a 'Book of Miscellanies' the difficulties of interpretation which he could not surmount, and the problems in theology which he could not immediately solve; and not unfrequently the solution came in maturer years.

One precious testimony of Boston's, more than once repeated by him even at this early period of his ministry, will find its echo in the heart of every devoted minister of Christ – that a heavenly frame of mind is the best interpreter of Scripture. There are great texts, especially those which belong to the region of Christian experience, which sound to the man of mere lexicons and grammars as paradoxes or riddles, and before which he will sit for days and weeks vainly guessing and groping at their meaning, but which sweetly open themselves almost at once to the mind which has 'tasted that the Lord is gracious', and disclose to him all their golden stores. It is a profound saying, expressing in another form Boston's meaning, that 'the best scriptural interpreter is the man with a scriptural mind.'

The Marrow of Modern Divinity

We have noticed the manner in which our young Simprin pastor hungered for books, and how scanty was his supply of this mental pabulum during the earlier years of his ministry. But there was one book to which we have now to advert which came into his possession without his seeking, even the name of which he had never before heard, which was destined to exercise over himself and his ministry a most powerful and benignant influence, and ultimately and partly through him, over the theological thinking and the ecclesiastical history of Scotland for ages to come. Other ministers, such as Mr. Hog of Carnock, soon became associated with him in his experience and action; but his was the hand which beyond all others put the leaven into the meal. This remarkable book was 'The Marrow of Modern Divinity'. Its author was Mr. Edward Fisher, a gentleman commoner of Brasenose College, Oxford. Its first part was published in May 1645, and its second part three years after; and it consisted largely of extracts from the writings of the Reformers and the Puritans, these having reference mainly to questions connected with the way of a sinner's access to God. We see the familiar names of Luther and Calvin and Beza shining out from the great multitude of honoured names, and the editor himself contributes an occasional sentence or brief passage. But he prefers to describe himself as one who has gathered sweet-scented and medicinal flowers from many a garden, and bound them together in one bunch of mingled sweetness and healing power. The book was strongly recommended by the famous Joseph Caryl, who held the office of censor of theological works, from the Westminster Assembly of Divines. And the fact that the entire work passed through ten editions in a few years after its publication, proves the avidity with which it was sought after and read.

The story of the manner in which the 'Marrow' found its way into this obscure corner of Scotland, and into Mr. Boston's hands, presents a remarkable instance of the unlikely means and the minute incidents by which God not unfrequently works out his great designs, especially for the advancement of his kingdom among men. How little did Luther dream when he found a copy of the Latin Bible in the Augustinian monastery at Erfurth, and began to read it, that he was 'the monk whom God had chosen to shake the world,' and that this discovery was to be the first step in his training for his glorious mission. The way of Boston's finding the 'Marrow', though greatly inferior in importance, belongs to the same class of providences. We shall best give the narrative of the finding of the 'Marrow' in Boston's own quaint words: 'As I was sitting one day in a house of Simprin, I espied above the window-head two little old books, which when I had taken down I found entitled, the one 'The Marrow of Modern Divinity', the other 'Christ's Blood Flowing Freely to Sinners'. These, I reckon, had been brought home from England by the master of the house, who had been a soldier in the time of the civil wars. Finding them to point to the subject I was in particular concern about, I brought them both away. The latter, a book of Saltmarsh's, I relished not, and I think I returned it without reading it quite through. The other, being the first part of the 'Marrow', I relished greatly, and purchased it, at length, from the owner, and it is still to be found among my books. I found it to come close to the points I was in quest of, and to show the consistency of these which I could not reconcile before, so that I rejoiced in it as a light which the Lord had seasonably struck up to me in my darkness.'

It is not difficult to understand how, in looking at the doctrine of election by itself, apart from the uses and connections in which it is presented in Scripture, Boston in his earlier years at Simprin should sometimes, to use his own words, have found himself confused, indistinct, and hampered in his proclamation to men of the free, open, and universal liberty of access to God in Christ for salvation. But when he was brought to see, from a hundred passages in the

'Marrow', that the gospel was the fruit and expression of God's love to every 'man of woman born', that 'God so loved *the world* that he gave his only begotten Son', or, to quote the words which became the recognized formula of 'Marrow' theology, that 'Jesus Christ was God the Father's deed of gift and grant unto all mankind lost', the morning mists passed away, he saw God's wondrous method of mercy in its full-orbed light and radiance, and began from that hour to sound 'the gospel trumpet's heavenly call' with a new energy and delight which his people and those in the surrounding parishes were not slow to recognize and relish. 'The time of the singing of birds had come.'

There is one statement in an early passage of his autobiography, probably having reference to this very period, in which our young minister describes himself as conversing with a visitor about 'the measure of humiliation requisite in a sinner before he can come to Christ.' If up to this time he had been hampered by this question, which has made so many to stumble and hold back on their way to Christ and peace, we may well believe that the teaching of the 'Marrow' would tell him how to deal with such an inquirer. He would insist on an immediate and unqualified closing with the message of heaven's love. He would assure the anxious one that he would never become better, but worse, by waiting. Why should you linger, even for a day, when the gate stands wide open, and the feast is ready, and the King is waiting with open arms to welcome you in? The only way to be made clean is to go to the fountain; the only way to be made warm is to go to the fire. In this way had Boston come to plead with men when preaching on such texts as 'Come unto me, all ye that labour and are heavy laden, and I will give you rest' – 'Ho, every one that thirsteth, come ye to the waters', on which the lamp of the 'Marrow' had shed a new light.

During the following fifteen years, the 'Marrow' doctrine spread far and wide over many of the fairest provinces of Scotland; it became incorporated with the preaching of not a few of its best ministers; and multitudes of sincere believers were so quickened by it that their experience seemed like a new conversion; while myriads of careless professors and open sinners entered with joy into the kingdom of the saved. There is truth in the remark that the

Marrowmen, first of all among our Scottish divines, entered fully into the missionary spirit of the Bible, and were able to see the Calvinistic doctrine 'was not inconsistent with world-conquering aspirations and efforts.'

Spiritual Blessing in Simprin

We return to our narrative. From the time that Boston had drunk of the reviving waters of the 'Marrow', his work in Simprin was carried on with increased freedom and crowned with greater success. Conscious that he had been put in trust with a divine message which was fitted for all, needed by all, and commanded to be proclaimed to all, he preached with an enlarged hope and earnestness. And Simprin was not only improved but visibly transformed. There was a new face upon everything. 'Instead of the thorn there had come up the fir tree, and instead of the brier there had come up the myrtle tree.' When he entered on his ministry in Simprin there was not a single house in which family worship was observed: within a period of less than seven years there was not a single home in all the parish without its family altar and its morning and evening sacrifice of praise and prayer. As it had been with Baxter at Kidderminster, when at the stated hours every house resounded with the voice of psalms, so it had come to be the experience of Boston in the cottages of this rural parish. And these are among the surest signs of thriving religious life among a people, just as there are certain flowers on the Alps which are sure to appear at a high elevation.

Moreover, in the later years of his Simprin pastorate, and especially on extraordinary communion occasions, multitudes came streaming from the neighbouring parishes to be 'present at the feast'; and many carried away with them in their hearts the memory of words and thoughts that never died, their awakened interest giving an increased enthusiasm and fervour to Boston's preaching, so that his lips seemed touched with hallowed fire, and he rose above himself. Writing in his diary at the recollection of one of those sacramental seasons, we find him testifying, 'If I ever preached, it was on that day'; 'I will ever remember Simprin as a field which the

Lord had blessed'.

In speaking of such successes as thus crowned and rewarded the ministry of Boston even at this early period, while we must look for the explanation mainly in the divine adaptation of the gospel and doctrine which he preached, we must look also at the personality of the preacher. Such a man preached to his people in his daily life. They beheld the witness to the divinity of his message, in its divine fruits, as he lived and moved before them. They could not doubt regarding such a man that he 'believed, and therefore spoke'. We have already quoted his own testimony that he preached his sermons to his own heart before he preached them to his people. And then they were studied in an element of prayer. His was the prayer ardent which

'Opens heaven, and lets down a stream
Of glory on the consecrated hour
Of man, in audience with the Deity.'

With what an intensity of gratitude do we find him recording in his diary instances of blessing in answer to prayer: 'My soul went out in love flames to the Advocate with the Father.'

This was emphatically a formative period in Boston's life. As an instance of this, we may mention the habit which he had already formed of daily meditation on the ways of Providence, especially in connection with his own spiritual life and ministry, and his extracting from these experiences the lessons which they suggested. By this means, the divine word and the divine ways were made to shed mutual light, and often the moral which they suggested was condensed into a proverb and preserved. In this manner his autobiography becomes even at this early stage of his life like his manse garden, a place abounding with wholesome fruits and medicinal plants. We shall enrich our narrative with a few of these:

'Spiritual decays suck the sap out of mercies.'
'There may be an enlargement of affection where there is a straitening of words.'
'The way of duty crossing people's way is a safe way.'

'When the Lord means a mercy to a people he helps them beforehand to pray for it.'

'A depending frame is a pledge of mercy desired.'

'Satan is sure to lay hold of us in a special manner when there is some great work that we have to do.'

'There is no keeping foot without new supplies from the Lord.'

Call from Ettrick

Early in the beginning of 1706, Mr. Boston was surprised by receiving the news of his having been called to be minister of the parish of Ettrick in Selkirkshire. It was not a welcome surprise. No doubt, Simprin was a little parish with a scanty population, by no means equal to his capacity of work and oversight; but during those seven years of his pastorate over that rustic flock, it had entwined itself around his affections. It was his 'first love'. There was not one among his parishioners whom he did not know, and the short and simple annals of whose family life, in which 'the dews of sorrow were lustred o'er with love,' which he could not have repeated. We are reminded of Goldsmith's lines:

'Even children followed with endearing wile
And plucked his gown, to share the good man's smile.'

And his ministry had been singularly blessed among them. They were indeed his 'living epistles'. How could he endure to be severed from a people who, in so many simple forms and ways, reciprocated his affection? Moreover, when the call from Ettrick came at length into his hands, 'his health', as he records in his diary, 'was so broken that he looked rather like one to be transported to another world than into another parish.' But still 'the Call' was there. It was a reality. It had come to him unsought and undesired. He was conscious in his own heart that he would not have so much as lifted up a finger to bring it forth; but now that it had come to him, he must look it full in the face, and endeavour to ascertain what was the will of his Master in heaven. Unbiassed by any poor ambitions or mercenary motives, this would be the only factor in determining his decision. He tells us that, 'leaving all in God's hands, he was willing from the first to go or stay as the Lord might give the word.' And 'when the eye was thus single, the whole body was full of light.'

At the same time, while he was thus prepared to obey the divine will, it was necessary that he should do his utmost to ascertain what this will was. He could not hope to hear a voice from heaven saying, 'This is the way, walk ye in it.' For this end he visited Ettrick, preached to the people, and sought by personal observation and otherwise to inform himself, especially regarding the moral and religious condition of the parish. Up to this time, his heart's preference had been to remain in Simprin. But what he saw and heard during those days in 'the Forest' made him hesitate, and even incline to make it the object of his choice, not because his work would be easy, but because the crying wants of the people were so great. 'The desolation in that parish,' he says, 'ever since I saw it, hath great weight on me, and I am convinced I should have more opportunity to do service for God there than here; but success is the Lord's.' Still, like Moses in the wilderness, who would not move with his myriad host until the pillar of cloud and fire moved, he would take no step until Providence gave its sign. 'The Lord helped me to believe that he would clear me in the matter in due time, and to depend on him for the same; while the word, "He that believeth shall not make haste," was helpful to me.' Well knowing, as he tells us, that 'several who had interest with God at the throne of grace were concerned to pray for light to him,' he at length determined to wait for the action of the synod in whose bounds the congregations both of Simprin and Ettrick were placed, and to accept its decision as the indication of the divine will.

And on the 6th day of March 1707, the synod having met, transferred Mr. Boston to Ettrick, a place with which his name has continued to be linked by many sacred associations in the minds of Christians throughout Scotland and in many other lands, up to the present day. Grey-headed elders were there from Simprin, weeping much at the thought of his being severed from them; and when he beheld their unfeigned grief, 'how,' says he, 'could my eyes fail to trickle down with tears?'

On the 1st day of May 1707, Mr. Boston was formally inducted as minister of Ettrick – a day, as he did not fail to note, remarkable in after ages as 'that in which the union of Scotland and England commenced according to the articles thereof agreed upon by the two Parliaments.' On the Sabbath after his admission, he began his ministry at Ettrick by preaching from the text 1 Samuel 7:12: 'Then Samuel took a stone, and set it between Mizpeh and Shen, and called the name of it Ebenezer, saying, Hitherto hath the LORD helped us.' It was not until the 15th day of June that he preached his farewell sermon to his Simprin people on John 7:37: 'In the last day, that great day of the feast, Jesus stood and cried, saying, If any man thirst, let him come unto me, and drink.' It was characteristic of the man to choose that grand evangelical text for such an occasion, when all the associations and incidents were likely to prepare and attune the hearts of the people for hearing. The multitude was very great, consisting not only of his sorrowing Simprin flock, but of thousands besides, who had come crowding from all the surrounding parishes to listen to a voice which the greater number of them knew they would hear no more. The place was at once a Bochim and a Bethel. He notices with glowing gratitude that 'the Lord who had been with him in his ministry there, was with him at the close, and much of God's power appeared in it.' It might have been said that 'that last day was the great day of the feast.' There was a holy awe over the hushed and expectant multitude; and though many a face that was turned to the preacher was suffused with tears, there was a prevailing element of joy which the text and the words which were spoken on it did not fail to produce and sustain. It was like the drawing of the loaded net by the disciples on the Sea of Galilee at the morning dawn, which they could scarcely drag to the land because of the multitude of fishes.

On the Thursday following, Mr. Boston with his wife and two children, Jane and Ebenezer, arrived at their new mountain home among the green hills of Ettrick. No doubt there were some momentary misgivings and regrets on that eventful day, but he was borne up by the consciousness that it was an overpowering sense of the divine call and leading that had brought him there. 'Thus,' says he, 'I parted with a people whose hearts were knit to me, and mine to them; nothing but the sense of God's command that took me there making me to part with them.' The times were not few in later years when he looked back with wondering gratitude, and even with fond heart-longings, upon his 'halcyon days at Simprin'.

We must not omit to mention that, in October 1702, Mr. Boston was chosen to the important office of Clerk to the Synod of Merse and Teviotdale, and that he held that office till 1711. Probably his suitableness for conducting the business of church courts had already in some measure revealed itself in the narrower sphere of his own presbytery, which was within the jurisdiction of the synod. The clerk's special duties were the recording of the proceedings of the synod in its minute-book, maintaining its correspondence with the presbyteries and sessions within its bounds, helping in the education and over-sight of students within the bounds of the synod who were preparing for the work of the Christian ministry; as well as the visiting of presbyteries and sessions in which the interference and advice of the synod were needed. Very different this from the routine duties of a quiet pastoral charge such as that to which he had been accustomed. But he did not shrink from the responsibility, all the more that the call to it had come unsought. Moreover, he knew that the works would only come to him at intervals; while perhaps he was not altogether unconscious that the parts of it which were most difficult were those for which he had a natural liking, and, as often happens in such cases, a peculiar fitness. His habits of order had been early formed. And the synod was not long in discovering that it had made a wise and happy choice. We find good men thus recording the traditions regarding him which they had received from his contemporaries: 'He had a great knowledge and understanding of human nature, of the most proper methods of addressing it, and the most likely handles for catching hold of it. And he had an admirable talent at drawing a paper.' We gather from passages in his diary that not unfrequently, when the synod was about to vote upon a question on which it appeared from the previous discussions there was not entire unanimity among the members, he succeeded in preparing such a minute as, by its happily-chosen words and well-balanced phrases, produced in the end entire harmony where, a little before, this issue had seemed very unlikely. But the testimony of Lord Minto, an eminent statesman, who had also been a judge, confirmed and exceeded all the others – that 'Mr. Boston was the best clerk he had ever known in any court, civil or ecclesiastical.'

5

MR. BOSTON'S FIRST TEN YEARS
IN ETTRICK

The parish of Ettrick is in the south-west of Selkirkshire. Its surface has been described as a 'sea of hills', which are finely varied in appearance, beautifully rounded at the top and covered with green grass to the summit. Some of its hills, such as Ettrick Pen, rise more than 2,000 feet above the level of the sea, and form part of the highest mountain range in the southern highlands of Scotland. Some centuries before the days of Boston, the whole of that tract of land which stretches along the margin of 'lone St. Mary's Loch', and, including both Ettrick and Yarrow, extends northward to the Tweed, was covered by the Ettrick forest. But now there is scarcely a straggling tree with its naked branches to suggest traditions of what once had been.

> 'The scenes are desert now and bare,
> Where flourished once a forest fair,
> When these waste glens with copse were lined
> And peopled by the hart and hind.'

But in the interval of less than two centuries, since the days of the good pastor of whom we are writing, what changes have come over Ettrick and its twin-sister Yarrow! Over the whole region there has been spread the mantle of romance, and it has become classic ground. In common with the lake district in Cumberland across the borders, where Wordsworth and Coleridge and Southey found a congenial retreat, and did much to enrich the literature of the world, this district of Scotland, with its green hills, and lonely glens, and sparkling streams, became the favourite haunt and home of poets. More than once Wordsworth was drawn to it from his own Rydal Mount and Grasmere, and in his 'Yarrow Visited' and Yarrow Revisited' he has owned the power of its fascination over him. Sir Walter Scott received impulse and inspiration alike from its scenery and its Border ballads and teeming traditions of war, and love, and chivalry, gradually becoming what Wordsworth called him in the enthusiasm of his admiration, 'the favourite of the world'.

But Ettrick claimed one as emphatically her own, as having been born and bred within her boundaries – James Hogg, the Ettrick Shepherd. His birth-place was in a half-ruined cottage in the little village of Ettrick, not far from the old parish church and its straggling retinue of trees. With no advantage of education or social position, with every influence against him except his indomitable courage and perseverance, and after many struggles and many failures, he rose at length to a first place among the poets of Scotland. His sphere was unique, but within it he was a master and stood unapproached. In expressing and depicting human passions and affections, Burns stood far above him; but in the region of pure imagination, especially in the world of the supernatural, he was in his element. In the beautiful picture of Kilmany, for instance, we feel, while reading, as if he must have actually lived with her in the enchanted land. In the hands of others who, in their own departments, are great poets, their supernatural characters are found after all to be real flesh and blood. But in such poems as the 'Queen's Wake' and others we are carried away to fairyland, and feel for a time as if we were in it. As has been happily said, 'we find ourselves walking in an enchanted circle, on a cloudless land, in a sunless world' (*Delta*).

But we must now turn back to the year 1711, and resume the story of him who, before the days of James Hogg, had made the name of Ettrick sacred, and won for himself also, by other and undying claims, the designation of the 'Ettrick Shepherd'.

Mr. Boston's first impressions of the people of Ettrick as he found them were not encouraging, but the reverse. Nothing indeed but the sense of his divine call to this new sphere and his faith in him who could 'make his strength equal to his day', could have kept him from fearing and even fainting at the prospect which opened before him. The discouraging causes came from more than one quarter. First, the parish had been without a minister, or the regular observance of the public ordinances of religion of any kind, for the previous four years. It was impossible that a people numbering many hundreds, and left for so long a time to wander as sheep without a shepherd, should not, in such circumstances, have greatly degenerated. The neglected and apparently forsaken parish had become morally and spiritually like an unploughed field which was covered with tangled weeds and thorns, and sheltered many foul creatures. The new minister notes in his diary, in his own characteristic manner and with observant sagacity, that 'he did not find the people's appetite for ordinances to have been sharpened by the long fast which they had got for about the space of four years; on the contrary, they were cold and indifferent about divine things, but keen about worldly gains to a proverb.'

Speaking of his parishioners in their characteristic moral features, and perhaps thinking the while of the quieter and less self-asserting people whom he had left behind him in the Merse, he describes them as 'naturally smart and of an uncommon assurance, self-conceited and censorious to a pitch, and using an indecent freedom both with church and state.' At the first, when he came among them, and for some time after, he was greatly shocked and discouraged by the indecent and disorderly behaviour of many of the people during divine worship, some of them rising with rude noise and seeming impatience, and others who had never entered the church, walking up and down in the surrounding churchyard with loud talking while the service was proceeding. So common was this unseemly outrage that two of the elders were at length appointed in rotation to watch against the offenders, and to see that no one withdrew from the church during the service without adequate reason, or occasioned noise and confusion around the church doors.

It was also not a little painful to the sorely-tried pastor to notice that, 'during his preaching', the majority among his hearers gave little heed to what was spoken on divine themes, but pricked their ears and were all attention when there was any allusion to public affairs, or to the current news of the day. Two other scandals filled up this dark and repulsive picture. One was the prevalence of profane swearing even among those who frequented public ordinances, 'the same fountain sending forth sweet and bitter', and the frequent occurrence among church members of sins and impurity, even in their grosser forms. When would this Augean stable be cleansed and turned into a temple of God? There was only one power in the universe that could do it.

Another circumstance which tended not a little, in the earlier years of Mr. Boston's Ettrick ministry, to disturb his peace and to hamper him in his work, was the presence in his parish of Mr. Macmillan, the minister and leader of a party among the Presbyterians who had refused to 'go in' with the Revolution Settlement of 1688, or to swear allegiance to the new dynasty which began with William of Orange. Without questioning the sincerity and conscientiousness of Mr. Macmillan and his followers, of whom there was a considerable number in the parish, it is easy to understand how their presence and constant agitation of points of difference in which Mr. Boston was the frequent object of attack, must have acted as an irritant upon his sensitive nature; while malcontents and fugitives from discipline were apt to seek refuge in the hostile camp. Still, in the face of all these frowning discouragements, he never regretted his having come to Ettrick; and while he may sometimes have thought of Simprin with a sigh, and written of himself in dark moments in his diary as 'like a bird shaken out of its nest, or an owl in the desert', he believed that a kindly hand was leading him amid the encircling gloom, and that the time was surely coming when 'at eventide there would be light.'

With these public trials in the first years of his ministry in Ettrick, there were mingled others of which the home was the scene. Within the brief period of eleven months, Mr. Boston was called to lay two infant children in the grave. After the custom of many of the Old Testament saints, who often made the name given to their children a memorial of blessings, or an expression of consecration and faith, he named the first-born of these Ebenezer, as at once a testimony of gratitude and an act of dedication. And when the second was born soon after the death of the first, the hallowed name was transferred to it with much earnest pleading in prayer that its young life might be spared. But it was not long ere sovereign Wisdom removed this little flower also to his upper garden. This second bereavement not only pierced the tender father's heart, but for a little time stumbled his faith, as if the dedication of his child had been rejected.

One scene in the death-chamber has been described by himself in words of pathos which can scarcely be read without tears: 'When the child was laid in the coffin, his mother kissed his dust. I only lifted the cloth off his face, looked on it, and covered it again, in confidence of seeing that body rise a glorious body. When the nails were driving, I was moved, for that I had not kissed that precious dust which I believed was united to Jesus Christ, as if I had despised it. I would fain have caused draw the nail again, but because of one that was present I resented and violented myself.' His later reflections reveal the riper fruits of his parental sorrow, and have been profitable to many who have been similarly called to hear 'deep calling unto deep'. 'I see plainly that divine sovereignty challenges a latitude, and I must stoop and be content to follow the Lord in an untrodden path; and this made me, with more ease, to bury my second Ebenezer than I could do my first. That Scripture was very profitable to me, "It was in my heart to build a house unto the Lord." I learned not to cry, How will the house be made up? but being now in that matter made a weaned child, desired the loss to be made up by the presence of the Lord.'

At length, the anxious pastor began to be cheered under his frowning discouragement, by being told of some who had spoken of his sermons as 'ripping up their case and discovering the secrets of their hearts.' This was like the plough snare turning up the hard soil for the reception of the seed. Those rousing sermons were seasonably followed by others unfolding to his hearers the divine method of salvation, the 'still, small voice' coming after the thunder and the tempest. In these there were already to be seen some of the germs of his 'Fourfold State', which, in due time, was to be given to the world, and to be one of the life-books of his own and succeeding ages, by means of which myriads were to be brought into the kingdom of God. Along with this, he associated catechetical lectures on Christian doctrine, as he had previously done in Simprin, using the Shorter Catechism as his text book, as had been the common practice some generations before among the English Puritans such as the saintly Flavel and others. And mingled with these were occasional sermons against the besetting sins of his parish, such as profane swearing and impurity; for he was not slow, when occasion called for it, to aim his winged arrows at a mark.

Alongside of Mr. Boston's ministry in the pulpit there were all the appliances of an enlightened and earnest pastorate – twice in the year catechizing groups of his people in the various districts of his parish, and once in the year visiting each of his families, like Paul at Ephesus, from house to house. In such a parish as Ettrick, extensive and mountainous, abounding also in mountain streams whose channels were often his only pathway, this part of his work proved to be laborious and dangerous, even when at length he provided himself with a pony. Moreover, it was no uncommon experience for him to be overtaken with darkness, or shrouded in mist, or arrested by a mountain stream which violent rains had rapidly swollen into the dimensions of a river and made for the time impassable. On some occasions, when he had become bewildered and lost his way, he would throw the bridle upon the neck of his sure-footed steed, and await until its sagacious instincts brought him once more upon known ground. Then would the gratitude of the saintly pastor, recognizing in all the hand of him without whom a sparrow cannot fall to the ground, find utterance in the suitable words of a psalm, and awaken, as he sang, the echoes of some lonely glen –

'Lord, thou preservest man and beast.
How precious is thy grace!
Therefore in shadow of thy wings
Men's sons their trust shall place.'

And so he persevered in this part of his sacred work, notwithstanding all its toil and peril, as making him better acquainted with the character of his people, with their modes of thinking, their spiritual wants, and their family history in its joy and sorrows; and thus giving him, as in the often remembered Simprin, a warmer place in their hearts, suggesting to him many a seasonable text for his sermons, doubling his moral influence, and making his 'pulpit the preacher's throne.'

Nor was he slow in surrounding himself at an early period with a body of Christian elders, who strengthened him much with their experience and friendly counsel, and aided him in many ways in the spiritual oversight of his flock, forming a living link between him and his people; helping him, moreover, in guarding the entrance of unsuitable members into the sacred fellowship of the church, and, by faithful discipline, in purifying the church from members who had proved themselves, by their ungodly and immoral lives, to be the servants of another master than Christ. The eldership is the strong point in the Presbyterian system, and the minister of Ettrick was not slow to recognize and appreciate the fact. In one page of his diary we find him giving relief to his affection for some of those elders who had 'obtained a good report', by embalming their names in glowing and grateful testimonies, as Paul writes of Gaius, and Aquila and Priscilla, and a whole constellation of workers who had 'helped him much in the Lord.' He speaks of one as 'a most kindly, pious, good man, and most useful in his office.' And he prays for another who, 'with his family, had been the most comfortable to him in his ministry. So it was all along, and so it continues to this day. May the blessing of God, whose I am, and whom I serve, rest on them from generation to generation. May the glorious gospel of his Son catch them early, and continue with them to the end, of the which I have seen some comfortable instances already.'

And he writes of yet another elder in the following words, in which the pen-portrait is traced with admirable discrimination: 'He was always a friend to ministers. Though he was a poor man, yet he had always a brow for a good cause, and was a faithful, useful elder; and as he was very ready to reprove sin, so he had a singular dexterity in the matter of admonition and reproof, to speak 'a word upon the wheels' so as to convince with a certain sweetness, that it was hard to take his reproofs ill.'

The Lord's Supper

It was not till more than three years after his settlement in Ettrick that Mr. Boston, with the advice of his elders, ventured to celebrate the Lord's Supper in his parish. It had long been a neglected ordinance, and like the Passover at one dark period in the history of the Israelites, had become 'as a thing out of mind'. But the faithful pastor knew that it was only those who were true disciples and could make a credible profession of their faith in Christ that had right and welcome to the sacramental feast, with all its thrice holy memories, and he concluded that his wisest course would be to reconstruct the congregation from the beginning. Acting on this conviction, he conversed, personally and alone, with every 'intending communicant'. And these interviews were designed, not only to act as a winnowing fan for separating the chaff from the wheat and so keeping the church pure, but for conveying instruction to the young inquirer, strengthening holy resolution, correcting mistakes, and suggesting rules and maxims for cheering the timid and guiding the inexperienced. Lessons and counsels given in such circumstances are likely to be remembered ever afterwards by the sincere disciple. The earnest Christian pastor, on such occasions intensely feeling the burden of the care of souls, may assure himself that he is not labouring in vain.

For weeks before, this man of God looked forward to the divine festival with anxious fears; but the nearer it came, he was the more carried above discouragement. He notes the fact that the sermons preached on the Lord's Day that preceded the communion seemed to have weight, and that he found his soul particularly pressed to follow that day's work with prayer. 'As for the work itself, it was more comfortable than I expected, and there seemed to be some blowings of the Spirit with it. I never saw a congregation,' he adds, 'more remarkably fixed and grave than they were. In all, there were about fifty-seven persons of our own parish communicants; few indeed, yet more than I expected amongst them.'

From that time onward, the Lord's Supper continued to be observed annually in the parish of Ettrick, and its recurrence became a sort of vantage-ground from which its minister could stand and look back, and measure the religious progress of his people from year to year. The heart of the anxious pastor watched for signs of the presence and working of the Holy Spirit among his parishioners as the husbandman watches for the rain-clouds to refresh his parched fields, or as the mariner looks up to the stars to guide his course; and year after year, he was cheered by tokens which sent him to his knees in thanksgiving. For though there was nothing as yet like a pentecostal effusion in which his whole parish, with its thousands, received a new life and impulse, and every individual was devoutly conscious of a baptism of fire, yet interest in divine things was deepening, the circle was widening, and there were conviction and anxious inquiry in many hearts. Men who had not observed the Lord's Supper for twenty years came seeking to handle and taste the sacred symbols of Christ's redeeming love, and those who had long been deserters of Christian ordinances in every form hastened to renew the times when it was better with them than now. Writing of the fifth of the annual communions, Mr. Boston records, in his own homely style of narrative, that 'there were 150 communicants who sat down at the sacred feast. At this time there were ten tables, though we used to have about seven, and the tables were longer than ordinary, and people came from a far distance.'

The Abjuration Act

The gratification which the true-hearted pastor derived from these signs of reviving life in his parish was disturbed by the action of Queen Anne's Parliament in framing an oath termed the 'Oath of

Abjuration', which was required to be taken by every minister of the church, on pain of his incurring a heavy and almost ruinous pecuniary penalty in the event of his refusal, and in case of his persistence in this refusal, his being compelled to vacate his pastoral charge. This startling and arbitrary decree naturally produced suspicion and alarm over the whole church. It was felt to be unnecessary as a pledge for the loyalty of men who, on their entrance on the ministry, had taken the oath of allegiance to the crown; and then its terms were so vague and ambiguous as to be perplexing to men of tender consciences, who could not be sure to what extent its language would commit them, and shut their mouths against faithful testimony-bearing, when the liberty and purity of the church might be tampered with by the civil power. The more ambiguous its terms, the more likely were they to conceal a snare. The oath was accordingly refused to be taken at all hazards by many of the best ministers, and not a few of those who bore the infliction with painful scruples deeply felt that 'an enemy had done this.' When the day of decision came, the fear of consequences held back the hands of the rulers from inflicting what would have been a most cruel and crushing penalty, and the pastor of Ettrick remained in possession of his manse and glebe.

And when, at a later period, it was attempted to make the oath more palatable by gilding it with some modifying clauses, Mr. Boston stood before his people prepared to suffer the loss of all things rather than sin, openly declaring in characteristic words that 'the oath could not be cleansed, and that, like the leper's house, it needed to be taken down.'

It remains, however, to be noticed that there were many among Mr. Boston's parishioners who had all along refused to believe that he would stand firm in the hour of decision, who even prophesied that at the end when he stood face to face with consequences he would swallow the obnoxious oath, and who watched and waited jealously for his fall. The heart of the anxious minister was pained by the knowledge of this. But they did not know the man, and judged of his conscience by their own pliancy when conscience and duty gave way before self-interest. But when the news came and spread over the parish that their minister had 'played the man in the fires', and had hazarded every worldly interest at the call of conscience, it was impossible any longer to withhold an involuntary approbation, and his moral power over the disaffected among his parishioners was increased from that day. It was one of God's movements for preparing the way for the wider triumphs of his servant's ministry in Ettrick.

Beyond the circle of his own mountain parish, Mr. Boston found encouragement and sympathy in some of the ministers in neighbouring parishes who, in the matter of Christian belief and religious experience, were like-minded with himself. It was the conscious unity of Christian brotherhood which, like a silent magnetic influence, drew them together, so that each was made stronger by the other. He had found this in his recent perplexities and troubles connected with the attempt to enforce upon ministers the Abjuration Oath. Among these 'brethren beloved' he names Mr. Henry Davidson of Galashiels and Mr. John Simson of Morebattle, whom he praises for 'his heavenly oratory', and Gabriel Wilson of Maxton, the last named of whom stood in the innermost circle of his affection. In his diary, he expatiates on his character with manifest delight, saying, with his keen perception and pleasing felicity of phrase: 'Whatever odds there was in some respects between him and me, there was still a certain cast of temper by which I found him to be my other self .... He was extremely modest; but once touched with the weight of a matter, very forward and keen, fearing the face of no man. In the which mixture, whereby he served as a spur to me and I as a bridle to him, I have often admired the wise conduct of Providence that matched us together.' It is worthy of remark that, ages after those excellent ones of the earth had ascended to their heavenly reward, their names continued to live in hallowed traditions in the parishes in which they had discharged a faithful ministry, and shed a halo upon their graves. 'The righteous shall be held in everlasting remembrance.'

Jacobite Rebellion

The sky of Providence seldom continues long without its clouds. After a brief and welcome interval, in which the heart of Mr. Boston was lifted up with joy by the signs of extending and deepening religious life in his parish, a new trouble suddenly arose to disturb the peace of the kingdom, in which Ettrick and its pastor were called to share. I refer to the outbreak of the rebellion in the latter end of August 1715, the design of which was to upset the present dynasty, and to place upon the throne of Britain a descendant of the exiled house of Stuart. A few sentences will be sufficient to explain how the good pastor and his people, dwelling among those remote hills and glens, were brought into unwelcome contact with this most unwise and reckless movement. The outbreak began with the Earl of Mar, who, at Braemar, in the north of Scotland, raised the standard of rebellion, and proclaimed the Pretender to be the rightful heir to the British throne. Immediately followed by other Highland chiefs and their clans, he began his march southward, obtaining numerous accessions on the way, until he reached Perth. Here it was determined by the rebel leaders that their army should be divided into several contingents, which, should march into England by different routes, and that one of the companies should proceed through the district in which Ettrick lay. It is at this point that Mr. Boston comes upon the scene. When the news became known, the effect was to produce an extensive panic over the whole region. Every new day brought with it its alarm. Companies of kilted Highlanders had been seen on the neighbouring hills. Others had been discovered skulking near quiet Ettrick homes after sunset, as if bent on mischief or violence of some kind. The alarmed people waited to hear of houses set on fire, or flocks scattered and slaughtered, or lonely dwellings entered and robbed, or human blood shed.

From week to week this panic continued, to the great distress of the anxious pastor. Then the trouble took a different form which vexed him with new anxieties. The local authorities sent forth a summons to every man in Ettrick from sixteen to sixty years of age, requiring him to appear in Selkirk on a certain day, in order to his being enrolled in a temporary militia for the defence of the parish; and Mr. Boston was required to read this summons from the pulpit, to produce and supply to the magistrates a roll of all the capable men in the parish, and to urge upon his parishioners universal obedience to the call. But there was a universal refusal. Many of the people had come to believe that the alarm was excessive, or that the dangers might be met by the forces which were already in the hands of their rulers, and probably also, unlike their ancestors in earlier generations, they held back. The men of Ettrick had learned to prefer the shepherd's crook to the sword. The popular resistance became all the more resolute when a tax was levied for the purpose of meeting the expenses that might be incurred in the anticipated conflict with the rebel invaders. It was a bitter cup which was thus given to Mr. Boston to drink; and one of the bitterest ingredients in it was that he was compelled to make the obnoxious communication to his parishioners, in whose affections he desired to live, the anger of the people falling far more upon him than upon its authors. The unreasonable estrangement, sometimes expressed in bitter words, was no doubt temporary, but while it lasted it was hard to bear.

At length the unwelcome insurgents, having been joined by the English rebels at Kelso, disappeared, and marched southward to Preston, of which they took immediate possession, and began to fortify it. But in a few days the place was invaded by General Willis, the leader of the royal troops, who soon compelled the rebels unconditionally to lay down their arms. Many of them were imprisoned, many persons of rank were subjected to a galling and ignominious treatment, and some who were Scottish noblemen were executed with a cruel severity.

We must look back to Scotland to behold the last scene in the drama. The Earl of Mar had meantime pressed forward to Dunblane, and there, on the neighbouring Sheriffmuir, he received a serious check from the Duke of Argyle, who had moved northward to resist his progress. When his affairs had become irretrievable and desperate, and when it was therefore too late to be of any service, the Pretender sailed for Scotland from Dunkirk in France, and, dressed in disguise, and with only six gentlemen in his train, landed not far from Aberdeen. Soon after, he was joined by the Earl of Mar and a little band of nobles and gentlemen at Fetteresso. For some weeks he spent his time in enacting the king, and received homage from his dispirited but devoted followers, without one shred of power to give the semblance of reality to the ceremonial. And then, weary of the ragged pageant, and declaring to those who had clung to him to the end with a wondrous chivalry his sense of the utter hopelessness of his enterprise, he set sail from the neighbourhood of Montrose in a small ship, accompanied by a few faithful adherents, arriving within five days at Gravelines in France, and returning to the obscurity from which he had so recently emerged. How rapidly had tragedy been turned into comedy and farce!

His Inner Life

It is time that we should now see something of Mr. Boston's inner life. During all those years of varied incident and experience which have passed under our notice in this chapter, he continued to maintain a close walk with God. His closet was his refuge and his sanctuary. Every event in his individual and family life was turned into food for devotion. Self-examination, sometimes accompanied with fasting, was his frequent practice, in which, as he tells us, he 'thought it safe and wise to antedate the judgment'. The records of some of these exercises which he has left behind in his diary are of singular value, and may be of use to some in our own days who perchance are seeking to know the truth and the worst about themselves. The following are some of his notes drawn from his own experience, on what he terms 'evidences for heaven':

'My soul is content with Christ for my king; and though I cannot be free of sin, God knows that he would be welcome to make havoc of my lusts and to make me holy. I know no lust that I would not be content to part with. My will bound hand and feet I desire to lay at his feet; and though it will strive whether I will or not, I believe that whatever God does to me is well done.'

'When may we be sure that afflictions are the evidences of God's love to us, and of our love to him? Though afflictions of themselves can be no evidence of the Lord's love, yet forasmuch as the native product of afflictions and strokes from the Lord is to drive the guilty from the Lord, when I find it not so with me, but that I am drawn to God by them, made to bless the Lord and accept the punishment of my iniquity, to love God more and to have more confidence in him and kindly thoughts in his way, and find my heart more closely cleaving to him, I cannot but think such an affliction an evidence of his love.'

I shall quote another passage descriptive of Mr. Boston's experience which belongs to the period of which I am now writing; not so much as a help to self-examination as for the purpose of 'comforting sorrowing hearts by the same comforts by which he was comforted of God.' It expresses a hope full of immortality, which made the cloud luminous and his heart submissive. His youngest child, Catherine, had died, and a thought was given to the tenderhearted father which had not been so present to his mind under any similar bereavement. He says: 'I never had such a clear and comfortable view of the Lord's having other uses for our children, for which he removes them in infancy, so that they are not brought into the world in vain. I saw reason to bless the Lord that I had been the father of six children now in the grave, and that were with me but a short time; but none of them is lost. I will see them all at the resurrection. That clause in the covenant, "I am the God of thy seed," was sweet and full of sap.'

By suggesting a similar thought a hundred years earlier, and in his own manse of Anwoth, Samuel Rutherford had helped others to drink at the same well of comfort. He thus writes to a bereaved mother weeping for her lost child: 'Do you think her lost who is sleeping in the bosom of Almighty love? Think not her absent when she is in such a Father's house. Is she lost to you who is found to Christ? Oh now, is she not with a dear Friend, and gone higher upon a certain hope that you shall in the resurrection see her again? Let our Lord pluck his own fruit at any season he pleaseth. They are not lost to you; they are laid up so well as they are coffered in heaven, where our Lord's best jewels lie.'

Reverting now to Mr. Boston's practice of self-scrutiny, and to the invaluable benefit which he derived from this, we think it necessary to introduce the qualifying statement that probably this habit of mental introversion was sometimes carried by him to excess, and that he 'wrote bitter things against himself without cause.' There were moods of spiritual depression which he ascribed to divine desertion, 'the hidings of his Father's countenance,' when perhaps, in some instances, the real cause of his mental gloom and sadness was to be found in a disordered body, or a shattered nervous system which needed to be restored by rest from excessive mental labour, or by change of scene, or by a bracing walk among his own Ettrick hills. When, as sometimes happened, the changes in his moods from cheerfulness to depression, or the reverse, took place more than once on the same day, fitful as the notes of the Æolian harp, might not the state of the body have had more to do with this than any spiritual cause, and might not the presence of the physician have been more needed than that of any spiritual counsellor? 'The silver bells were all out of tune.' There was something suggestive in the acknowledgment of an eminently good man that 'he had least enjoyment in his religion when the wind was in the east.' There are times when the innocent sufferer sees –

'Too clearly, feels too vividly, and longs
To realize the vision with intense
And over-constant yearning – there, there lies
The excess by which the balance is destroyed.'

Of course, where the man's conscience accuses him of recently contracted sin, or the voluntary exposure of his heart to blighting spiritual influences, or the partial neglect of the means of grace, the explanation is to be sought in the sense of divine displeasure, when the daughters of music in the soul are brought low. The same depression of spirit having its root in the same physical cause, and leading our good pastor to form mistaken and unfavourable conclusions about himself, occasionally showed itself in his imagining that the divine blessing was being withheld from his ministry, and that like the mountains of Gilboa on which the curse of barrenness fell, the dew of heavenly grace had ceased to fall upon his heaven-sent message. He has himself left behind him in his diary the record that, in one instance, after the interval of a few days, the bruised reed was revived, and the gentle rebuke from heaven for his dark thoughts came in the news of multitudes of his people consciously quickened and gladdened as with a fresh soul-baptism by those very sermons which had seemed to him as 'water spilt upon the ground.' But those moods of depression were comparatively rare experiences. We find him more frequently recording happy weeks of a heavenly life.

We now pause for a moment to cull from this period of Mr. Boston's biography some of those semi-proverbial sayings which grew out of his Christian experience during his first decade in Ettrick. Some of these, as we have found in earlier quotations, are medicinal plants, others are sweet-scented flowers:

'Unto the trials which God brings in men's way, they often add much of their own which makes them far more weighty and bulky than otherwise they are in very deed.'

'Satan watches to prevent the good of our afflictions: how much need is there to watch against Satan.'

'I saw it was vain to empty the heart of what was its carnal choice, unless it was filled with something better than what was taken from it.'

'I have often found it good to follow duty over the neck of inclination.'

'I endeavoured to antedate my reckoning with my Judge.'

'It is the usual way of Providence with me that blessings come through several iron gates.'

'They have great need to take heed to their feet who are let within the veil, for our God is a jealous God.'

'I have found the Lord easy to be entreated, and recovery to be got without long onwaiting.'

'Melancholy is an enemy to gifts and graces, and a great friend to unbelief.'

In 1715, Mr. Boston found time, at the urgent request of many of his ministerial friends, to publish a little book under the title of the 'Everlasting Espousals', the flower of his people, who had probably heard the substance of the book in the form of a sermon or sermons, heartily seconding the request. It was founded on Hosea 2:19-20, and was the heavenly Bridegroom's address to his bride the church. 'I will betroth thee unto me in righteousness, and in judgment, and in loving-kindness, and in mercies. I will even betroth thee unto me in faithfulness: and thou shalt know the LORD.' It was his maiden publication since he became a minister, the first sheaf in a long and continuous harvest of religious books which he was to give to the church, and in which were already to be seen more than one of the characteristic excellences of his later and riper works. Among other things, its publication gave him an opportunity of testing his acceptance as an author with the Christian public. And the result was encouraging. Within comparatively short intervals, the little volume passed through three editions, finding many readers far beyond the glens of Ettrick, especially in Edinburgh, who were not slow to express their desire for a greater number of refreshing draughts from the same newly-opened fountain. And who can tell but that such communications as these may have given hint and impulse to the preparation of that *opus magnum* which was, in a large measure, to engross the thoughts and anxieties of his life. He felt that his mission was not to build a house for himself but a temple for God.

It falls to be noticed here that a few years before the time of which we are now writing, a Hebrew Bible had come into Mr. Boston's hands, upon the study of which, assisted by Cross's 'Tagmical Art', he entered with an enthusiasm and zest which continued with him to the end of his life. There was no dryness to him in those Hebrew roots of which the author of 'Hudibras' complained in his day. Even the mystery which hung about the 'accents' charmed him. At the period of which we are now writing he met with another learned work, by Wasmuth, on Hebrew accentuation, which quickened his curiosity, and made that a delight to him of which many soon have wearied. He seemed to himself always to be on the verge of some new discovery. Unquestionably these inquiries, into which he threw his whole heart, served as a useful mental alternative in connection with his weekly preparations for the pulpit. And he never hesitated to affirm that they shed much new light to him on many parts of the Old Testament scriptures. He even hoped that he would, by persevering research and thought, be able to help in solving some of those problems in that branch of sacred literature which were perplexing scholars both on the continent of Europe and in the English universities. We shall meet with the Hebrew 'accents' again.

Call to Another Parish

We have now to notice an event of no little moment, both in itself and in its consequences, in the history of Mr. Boston and his parish. In the month of September 1716, a call was addressed to the pastor of Ettrick by the church and parish of Closeburn in Dumfriesshire, inviting him to become their minister. This was soon after followed by the appearance of commissioners from Closeburn and the presbytery to which it belonged, urging upon him the claims of the church in Nithsdale, especially on account of the largeness of the congregation and its distracting divisions, which, it was believed, the ministry and oversight of Mr. Boston would be sufficient to heal; while it was more than hinted that the stipend would exceed that of his present charge. The same unwelcome strangers were also seen by the quick-sighted parishioners, once and again visiting the manse at Ettrick; and their errand was readily guessed.

All this filled the mind of Mr. Boston with anxiety and alarm, and drove him to his wonted and unfailing resource of prayer. But from the first, he was strongly averse to his removal from Ettrick. His heart and his conscience alike rose against the thought of his leaving that people 'as sheep without a shepherd,' notwithstanding much that had happened to chill his affection and loosen the bonds that had bound him to them. He thought of the spiritual desolation which he had found among them nine years before when he had come to be their minister; of the little flock which he had gathered around in the first years of his anxious labours; and how, in the nearer interval, and in the face of much and varied discouragement and opposition, it had increased by hundreds. But he thought also of their inexperience and imperfection, with scarcely any man among them qualified to lead them at such a crisis as his removal would be certain to produce; and he was convinced that the certain effect of his leaving them at such a time would be to undo much of his work in all the past, while it would be the signal to those who were watching for their halting and discord, and ready to enter in like ravening wolves to bite and devour.

Moreover, the good pastor, with his keen observation and moral sensibility, could not overlook the likelihood that, in the event of his accepting the invitation which held out to him the promise of larger emolument and higher social position, his Ettrick people would ascribe his action to mercenary motives; the moral power of his past life among them would thus be withered in a night, and the character of the Christian ministry would suffer at his hands. He therefore determined that nothing would tear him from Ettrick, already sacred to his heart by many hallowed associations and tender memories, but the distinct indications of Providence that this mountain home was no longer to be his rest.

And the state of mind and action of his people did much to confirm him in this conviction and resolution. The value with which they saw their pastor regarded by others did much to heighten their own estimate of his excellence; and blessings are likely to acquire a higher price in our estimate when they seem about to be lost. Even little and undesigned incidents sometimes revealed much to the observant minister, who was a thoughtful student of the book of Providence – as when he was walking one day along the public road with one of the elders from the competing congregation in Nithsdale, some poor women meeting them on the way, and fearing how all these visits and interviews might end, stood still and wept aloud. One of the wealthiest heritors in his parish, who had up to that time remained disaffected and never entered his church, now began to attend with regularity on the public ordinances of religion, and continued the practice to the end of his life. And many whom he had comforted in times of sickness or sorrow, or helped in their struggles with poverty, or won back to Christ from a life of ungodliness or vice, came to plead with him, even with tears from eyes unwont to weep, to remain among them. At length a fast was proclaimed, to which multitudes not only of communicants but of parishioners came, swelling the stream of worshippers from every quarter in Ettrick, that they might avert, by confession of sin and prayer, the threatened deprivation. It was impossible that the love to Ettrick and its people of this man of simplicity and godly sincerity should not have been greatly strengthened and riveted by these natural and unforced utterances of their veneration and attachment.

We shall not minutely trace the history of the 'call', in which Closeburn, 'coveting earnestly the best gifts', sought to unsettle Mr. Boston's connection with Ettrick and to obtain him as its pastor, and Ettrick, with awakened enthusiasm, did its utmost to retain him whom the very effort had not unnaturally led it to value more than ever. It would be a dreary and tangled narrative were we to describe the call in its various stages in sessions, and presbyteries, and synods, 'dragging its slow length along' through a period of nearly twelve months. We shall come at once to its final issue before the Commission of the General Assembly in 1717, to which its settlement was committed. Learned advocates, according to the custom in such cases, had already spoken on either side, and when their dialectics were ended, the minister of Ettrick, who was the most deeply interested, and, so far at least as Ettrick was concerned, knew the facts and merits of the case best, rose and asked permission to speak. Naturally bashful and timid, yet when he was moved by a sense of duty, he rose above the fear of man; while his yearning love for his people, from whom he dreaded the very thought of being severed, made him speak with a holy fervour and a tender persuasiveness as if his lips had been touched with celestial fire. We have only space for a few closing paragraphs:

'Moderator, will the justice of the Reverend Commission allow them to lay a congregation desolate which was planted with so much difficulty, has been managed with so much uneasiness, and upon the event of this transportation must become the very seat of separation in the country, and which there is so little hope of the comfortable supply of, they in the meantime so vigorously reclaiming, and all this in a time wherein there is so very little need of transportations, but the parish pursuing may be otherwise settled to far greater advantage? Will their respect to the peace of this church suffer them to give such ground of irritation to a congregation in the circumstances I have narrated? Will their compassion allow them to take one whose spirit is already shattered with the effects of this divisive temper, and cast him into another place where it must be far more so or to lead out one and set him upon the ice where he knows no way how to keep his feet, and when he falls must fall for nought – I mean, no advantage to the church gained thereby. Nay, Moderator, I cannot believe these things.

'I have been twice settled already, and I bless the Lord who was pleased in both convincingly to show me his own call coming along with the call of his church. And I have felt so much need of the former, its accompanying the latter, that it would be most inexcusable to venture on removing to another parish without it. I was persuaded in my conscience of the Lord's calling me to Ettrick, and my clearness as to my call to that place was never overclouded, no, not in my darkest hours; and had I not had that to support me there, I had sunk under my burden. Now, I have endeavoured, according to the measure of the grace bestowed on me, to set aside my own inclinations and the consideration of the ease and satisfaction of my own heart, and to lay this matter before the Lord for light, to discover his mind about it, labouring to wait upon him in the way of his word and works. But I sincerely declare after all, that I have no clearness to accept the call to Closeburn, nor a foundation for my conscience in this transportation, which ought not to rest on human authority. I have all deference for the authority of this church, and my ministry is very dear to me; so I cast myself at your feet, begging that you will not grant this transportation, which has been refused by the presbytery and synod whereof I am a member, and who are best acquainted with the state of the parish of Ettrick and what concerns me, whereas both that parish and I are known but to very few of our now reverend judges. But if it shall please the holy wise God to suffer me, for my trial and correction, to fall under your sentence transporting me from the parish of Ettrick to the parish of Closeburn, since it is a charge I have no clearness to undertake, I resolve, through grace, rather to suffer than to enter on it blindfolded. Though, in the meantime, I cannot help thinking it will be hard measure to punish me because I cannot see with other men's eyes.'

When Mr. Boston began his speech, the impression among the members of the Commission itself, as well as among onlookers, was that by far the preponderating majority of votes would be in favour of his translation to Closeburn. But as he proceeded in his arguments and appeals, it was not difficult to read in the countenances of many of the reverend fathers that they were becoming unsettled in their preferences, and that the vote would finally fall on the side of Ettrick. And so it turned out to be. 'By a vast majority,' the grateful man himself reports, 'the sentence passed in our favour; and others as well as I were convinced that the speech I delivered was that which influenced the Commission and moved their compassion.... I must say that the Lord was with me in the management, giving me in that hour both what to speak and courage to speak it; and even when I ran, he left me not to stumble.'

The good tidings carried joy into every farmhouse and shepherd's shieling and poor man's cottage in Ettrick. We can imagine bonfires to have been kindled on every mountain throughout the wide parish, such as the men of a few generations back were wont to kindle when the people had heard of an invasion from the other side of the Border. On the following Sabbath the church could not contain more than a fraction of the multitudes that came from every quarter of the parish to thank God for the happy termination of their months of anxiety. The event marked an epoch, not only in Mr. Boston's life and ministry, but in the religious history of the parish. Coldness and distrust seemed to have vanished. By that disinterested act, in which he had so earnestly pleaded for his retention in Ettrick, he had placed his noble unselfishness beyond doubt, and revealed a love to his people which many waters could not quench. He had won the hearts of all. The people now understood their minister. The personality of the man would henceforth more than ever enhance the power of his message. He had the consciousness that he was now to preach to a united people, and it was not long ere his increased influence and usefulness began to show themselves in many forms. He did not flatter himself that he would never again meet with inconsistencies among his people, and even discouraging falls. But it was now, in comparison with much of his past experience, as if the ship had passed outside the region of frequent storms, and were sailing calmly before the trade-winds to the destined haven.

6

GROWING INFLUENCE

With the affection and confidence of his parishioners now gathered around him, and delivered from the distracting and depressing cares produced by division and alienation, Mr. Boston now proceeded to the composition of his 'Fourfold State', with which his own name and that of Ettrick were to be permanently and indissolubly associated. It is probable that the writing of the book did not occupy more than two years in the earlier part of the second decade of his Ettrick ministry, but from various causes long intervals of years intervened more than once to hinder further progress, and almost indefinitely to arrest publication. Moods of self-diffidence again and again held him back from this decided step; and a desire to bring the book nearer to his ideal of what it ought to be, when treating of themes of such transcendent importance and interest, had greatly increased delay. In addition to this, his modest estimate of the probable success of his book, along with his knowledge of his scanty income, made him dread pecuniary difficulties in case of failure. But this impediment, as it became known, was promptly met by the promise of all necessary help from those brethren in the ministry whom we have already named, and whose appreciation of the author and his book was very much higher than his own. As for Dr. Trotter, his 'beloved physician' and 'inner friend' both at Simprin and Ettrick, who had thrown out the first hint of writing such a book as the 'Fourfold

State', and who loved him with all the chivalrous affection of Jonathan to David, he would have been ready, out of his own resources alone, to meet all difficulties; but he had died during those irritating and irksome delays. And so a publisher in Edinburgh was at length sought for and secured, and the printing of the 'Fourfold State' proceeded with.

At the very beginning, however, an incident occurred, not without its ludicrous features, but which must have sorely tried the temper and strained the patience of the much-enduring pastor. It appears that one of the civic dignitaries of Edinburgh had, in some way or other, assisted in business negotiations connected with the procuring of a suitable printer and publisher of the 'Fourfold State'. But not satisfied with this act of kindness, which would have been of some use to the author, he had spontaneously offered the further and unsought service of revising the proof-sheets of the book as it passed through the press, making his amendments and suggestions immediately after they had passed from the printer's hands, and before they had been sent out to Ettrick. And in his overweening self-conceit, this gratuitous censor had imagined that his revision was to extend, not only to the accuracy of the printer, but to the style and even to the thought of the author, so as to introduce foreign sentences, or portions of sentences, into the composition. What, then, must have been the astonishment and mortification of Mr. Boston when he found the first proof-sheet, as revised by the city Treasurer, blotted and blurred all over with corrections, and changes introduced which extended not only to printers' blunders but at times to sentiment and style, toning down pithy sayings into vapid inanities, or substituting magniloquent commonplace for strong words of fearless earnestness, which were meant and fitted to arouse and alarm the conscience. It was like advising a racer to mend his pace by mounting upon stilts, or putting into a warrior's hand a sword that was wrapped in ivy. This presumption was too much even for the endurance of the Ettrick pastor. Sending to the printer for clean 'proof', he intimated at the same time to his too officious patron that he would dispense with his further aid.

This practice of using unjustifiable liberties with authors and their writings did not die out with Boston's age. The poet Montgomery, who did so much to enrich by his hymns the hymnology of the churches, complained that, in many instances, the compilers of hymn-books not content with receiving from him liberty to appropriate his hymns without any remuneration, altered them at their pleasure, and almost always for the worse, destroying the rhythm and cadence of the lines, substituting some prosaic word for an expression that had a picture in it, and sometimes not only changing the thought but making the author say what he did not believe.

The comprehensive and felicitous title of the book was in these words, 'Human Nature in its Fourfold State of Primitive Integrity, Entire Depravity, Begun Recovery, and Consummate Happiness of Misery'. This sufficiently indicated that the author was to present his readers with a complete system of Christian theology, intended to describe the divine method of human redemption, to be a compact statement of 'the glorious gospel of the blessed God', to show that way back from 'Paradise lost' to Paradise regained'.

There was one important and outstanding feature of the book in which the author's manner of treatment distinguished it from the greater number of those systems of theology which had been given to the world both in his own and in earlier times. Those systems were usually too scientific in their structure and style for common readers, being overlaid with learning, deficient in the practical element, and too often also rendered repulsive by distracting and unprofitable controversy about comparative trifles. The aim of the pastor of Ettrick, who was brought into daily contact with the common people and knew their modes of thinking and feeling, was, while presenting Christian truths in systematic form, and in such a manner as to show their mutual relation and dependence, to adapt his language to the general capacity of his readers, and to bring the whole to bear upon men's greatest wants and their eternal well-being. As has been happily said, 'He took the bewildered child of trespass familiarly by the hand, and descending to the level of his untutored capacity, gave him a clear and consecutive view of the innocence from which he had fallen, the misery in which he was involved, the economy of restoration under which he was situated, and the hope which, by submitting to that economy, he might warrantably entertain. His eye, as he wrote, was upon the unawakened sinner, that he might arouse him from his dangerous lethargy; upon the anxious inquirer, that he might guide his steps into the right way; and upon the young convert, that he might guard him against devious paths and perilous delays. He never failed to show the bearing of Christian doctrine upon the conscience, the affections, and the life, and to mingle with the light of systematic arrangement beseeching tenderness and practical appeal' (*the late Dr. Young of Perth*).

Once and again, while reading the 'Fourfold State', we have been struck with the author's felicitous application of Scripture sentences, so fitting them to surrounding circumstances as if they had been placed in the Bible for that very occasion. In like manner, we have been charmed with his skilful adaptation of Scripture incidents to passing events, and also with the ingenuity with which he struck new thoughts out of familiar texts, having all the effect of a new discovery, or of a pearl found upon the trodden highway; and all this expressed in happily chosen words like 'apples of gold in baskets of silver', reminding us of Philip Henry in his more genial and happy moods. While, at other times, we have been astonished when he has seemed to read our very heart, and to give a wondrous reality to the things which are unseen and eternal and we have felt as if he had inherited the rare power of Richard Baxter as seen in his 'Now or Never' and his 'Saint's Everlasting Rest'.

We have Mr. Boston's own testimony, more than once repeated in his diary, that his 'Fourfold State' was written throughout in connection with much prayer. And there is a tradition which can be traced up to his own times, that the last chapter of his book, on the congenial subject of Heaven, was literally written by him on his knees. And when we read that part of the book, the tradition becomes the more credible. There is a singular elevation in his thoughts and grandeur in his words which transcends all that had been previously written. It then seems as if, like Bunyan's Pilgrim, he had been walking in the land of Beulah, had seen the angels, and heard the sound of the heavenly minstrelsy. The following are his words on Mutual Recognition in Heaven:

'There we shall see Adam and Eve in the heavenly paradise, freely eating of the tree of life; Abraham, Isaac, and Jacob, and all the holy patriarchs, no more wandering from land to land, but come to their everlasting rest; all the prophets feasting their eyes on the glory of Him of whose coming they prophesied; the twelve apostles of the Lamb sitting on their twelve thrones; all the holy martyrs in their long white robes, with their crowns on their heads; the godly kings advanced to a kingdom which cannot be moved; and them that turn many to righteousness shining as the stars for ever and ever. There shall we see our godly friends, relations, and acquaintances, pillars in the temple of God, to go no more out from us.

'And it is more than probable that the saints will know one another in heaven – that, at least, they will know their friends, relatives, and those they were acquainted with when on earth, and such as have been most eminent in the church. This seems to be included in that perfection of happiness to which the saints shall be advanced there. If Adam knew who and what Eve was at first sight, when the Lord God brought her to him, why should one question that husbands and wives, parents and children, will know each other in glory? If the Thessalonians, converted by Paul's ministry, shall be his "crown of rejoicing in the presence of our Lord Jesus Christ at his coming", why may not one conclude that ministers shall know their people, and people their ministers in heaven? And if the disciples on the Mount of Transfiguration knew Moses and Elias, whom they had never seen before, we have ground to think that we shall know them too when we come to heaven. The communion of saints shall be most intimate there: "they shall sit down with Abraham, Isaac, and Jacob in the kingdom of heaven". Lazarus was "carried by the angels into Abraham's bosom", which denotes most intimate and familiar society.'

On November 6, 1720, Mr. Boston received from his publisher in Edinburgh the first bound copy of his 'Fourfold State'. The next morning, he remained for many hours in his study engaged in continuous thanksgiving and in prolonged prayer. Not long before, he had written this record in his diary: 'I had much to stand the thought of publishing that book, being tossed betwixt two, namely, venturing such a mean piece into the world, while many, whose books I was not worthy to carry, are silent; and the fear of sitting the call of Providence.' But in a few months, the heart of the too diffident author was cheered by the news from Edinburgh of the rapid sale of a second and even a third edition. And years before his death, he was able to record, with mingled humility and thanksgiving which rose to adoring wonder, that the treatise had won the hearts of all classes and conditions of men. We have already noted, in our introductory remarks, that by means of his 'Fourfold State', which he had hesitated for years to launch on the uncertain sea of public opinion, Mr. Boston was virtually preaching the gospel of heaven's great love, not only to his people in Ettrick, but to the south and south-eastern provinces of Scotland. In all the counties watered by the Tweed, the Nith, the Annan, the Dee, and the upper districts of the Clyde, it was literally read by all, and converts were made by thousands.

We find him mentioning in the last chapter of his diary that, far beyond the sphere in which the 'Fourfold State' had borne its earliest harvests, he had received a 'comfortable account' of its acceptableness and usefulness in remote places, particularly in the Scottish Highlands. And not only in the cottages of the poor and in the homes of the middle classes, but equally in the mansions of the wealthy and in the castles of the noble, it was welcomed, and came with healing on its wings. On the little book-shelf in the lonely cottage in remote glens it lay a cherished thing side by side with Bunyan's immortal allegory. And this continued through more than one or two generations. It was one of those books which God had chosen by which to work his miracle of grace. Even the everyday conversation of the common people came at length to be enriched by many of those proverbial and pithy sayings with hooks upon them, in which the 'Fourfold State' abounds. Its frequent and delighted perusal made many of them not only enlightened

Christians, but able theologians; and even ministers of religion of a certain class, who were more familiar with current literature than with the epistles of Paul, have been known, in disputing on religious questions with those Border wrestlers, to receive an ugly fall. It would be impossible for any man fitly to write the religious history of Scotland during the greater part of the eighteenth century and the earlier part of the nineteenth, without acknowledging that, during all that long period, this book had been one of the mightiest factors in leading men into the kingdom of God. It is not even at this day an exhausted power.[1]

Communion Seasons in Ettrick

There was another new experience which began to yield much holy enjoyment to the heart of Mr. Boston, and which probably continued to gladden his spirit to the end of his life. I refer to the multitude of people who came in streams from other parishes, and even travelled from distant parts of Scotland, to be present at the annual observance of the Lord's Supper, and to join with the Ettrick worshippers in the week of holy festivities that were associated with it. This practice found its explanation, not only in the attraction of Mr. Boston's eminent gifts as a preacher, as well as of other ministers of kindred spirit whom he was accustomed to associate with him in those annual gatherings, but also, and even yet more, in the fact that, in too many of the parishes of Scotland, ministers had begun to preach 'another gospel which was not another', and to substitute the husks of a shallow and sapless philosophy, or of dry moralities, for that divine message which they had been commissioned to preach, and by which God saves souls; and that their dissatisfied hearers came crowding annually to those communion festivals like thirsty pilgrims in a desert to a fountain of living waters, often beguiling the tediousness of the journey and making the glens and mountain-sides vocal by the singing of psalms:

---

1. *Editor's note*: The book is still in print today, published by the Banner of Truth, Edinburgh, Scotland.

'They chant their artless notes in simple guise;
They tune their hearts – by far the noblest aim:
Perhaps "Dundee's" wild warbling measures rise,
Or plaintive "Martyrs", worthy of the name;
Or noble "Elgin" beets the heavenward flame –
The sweetest far of Scotia's holy lays.'

It often reminded them of the Jewish pilgrims in Old Testament times ascending in companies to Jerusalem to keep their Passover.

Mr. Boston welcomed those annual visitors as if he had heard the words of an apostle, 'Be not forgetful to entertain strangers, for thereby some have entertained angels unawares.' He led the van in the ever-enlarging hospitality which extended over many days; at length adding, at his own expense, two new and spacious rooms to his manse, for the increased accommodation of strangers, many of whom he knew to be true brethren in Christ, and others earnest inquirers after the way of life, and not far from the kingdom of heaven.

And the happy Ettrick people were in full sympathy with their minister, with enlarged hearts more and more devising liberal things. There was more than one Phebe, or Gaius, or Priscilla in those lonely glens and beside those mountain streams, waiting and longing to give full scope to their hospitality and love. Mr. Boston writes of one Isabel Biggar, 'a singular Christian', as on one occasion 'entertaining a great weight of strangers'. And, writing of another week of sacred festival, he places it on pleasant record that 'in the one district of Midgehope alone there were about ninescore strangers, fourscore of whom were entertained by William Blaik, husband of Isabel Biggar aforesaid'; adding, with homely detail, 'having before baken for them half a boll of meal for bread, bought four shillings and tenpence sterling of wheat bread, and killed three lambs, and made thirty beds. And I believe their neighbour, Robert Biggar, Isabel's brother, would be much the same. This I record, once for all, for a swatch of the hospitality of the parish; for God hath given this people a largeness of heart to communicate of their substance on these and other occasions also. And my heart has long been on that occasion particularly concerned for a blessing on their substance, with such a natural emotion as if they had been born of my body. Those within a mile of the church still had the far greater weight on solemn occasions.'

There are reasons for thinking that it was at this period that Mr. Boston began the practice of setting apart a fixed proportion of his annual income for religious and benevolent objects, acting in the spirit of Paul's direction to the members of the church at Corinth: 'On the first day of the week, let every one of you lay by him in store as God hath prospered him.' Dr. Paley, and others in his times, have been credited with being the first to hold up this apostolic suggestion to the notice and imitation of the churches; but the practice had long before been anticipated, at least in its principle and spirit, by the good pastor of Ettrick. The words in which he records this, in writing to his family, are characteristic in their minuteness of detail, and they mark the beginning of a practice which was cheerfully continued to the end of his life:

'A part of my stipend coming in about that time, I did, on the 30th March 1718, lay by fifty merks thereof for pious uses. And all along since that time I have kept a private box, making up into yearly portions the said sum of fifty merks; laying it in mostly by parcels, and giving out of it as occasion requires, and I always keep of it in my left side pocket. The dealing to the poor at the house for their food continues as formerly without respect to this; only what wool is given them in the summer, since I have none of my own, is bought out of this fund; out of which also our Sabbath's contributions are taken. This course I have found to be profitable to the poor, and affording much ease to myself; for I have thereby been in case to give considerably on special occasions, and that with more ease to myself than otherwise I could have had, always looking on that part of my yearly income as not mine, but the Lord's.'

It will be noticed that in those words the good pastor not only states the commencement of this practice, but his satisfaction in it after some experience. It secured deliberation and system in his giving, and rendered it more likely that his income would both be laid aside and distributed under religious influence and motive. It guarded him alike against improvident excess and grudging restraint, when conscience and charity were joined hand in hand in the stewardship of his worldly means. And it even helped to foster a healthful religious spirit when looking at his annual deposits, in thinking of them as consecrated things, which were no more his than the gift of the worshipper in the temple after he had laid it on the altar of God.

In the midst of these notices of events and experiences, which must have opened many a spring of gratitude and joy in the heart of this devoted minister of Christ, we are now called to mention one event which became to him a life-long source of anxiety and sorrow. In the summer of 1720, his beloved wife, whose character we found him depicting, at an early period of his married life, with so much glowing appreciation and beauty, began to show unmistakable symptoms of insanity. To quote his own words, 'Her imagination was vitiated in a particular point, to her great disquietment, accompanied with bodily infirmities and maladies exceeding great and numerous.' And this dark eclipse of the spirit, though sometimes diminished, seldom wholly passed away; while in later years the gloom became darker still. The once sweetly-sounding lute sent forth only discords. It touched Mr. Boston on his tenderest point. Certainly, if he had been allowed, like David, to choose between various forms of suffering, this was the last which he would have chosen. At length the dear sufferer was confined entirely to one apartment, which her husband touchingly called 'the inner prison', and there she spent months and years, the subject of a mental malady which no science or human device could even mitigate. Allusions to this great sorrow appear again and again in Mr. Boston's diary, and as we read them we seem to hear his groans and sighs. Was this the Refiner's fire into which he had once more cast his gold for its seventh refining? His ministry and work, along with his unfailing resource of prayer, brought the sufferer his best relief. The affliction was one of those mysteries of Providence to which many of God's saints are no strangers, and which wait for the explanations of that glorious world where 'in God's light we shall see light'.

7

HOME LIFE, STUDY, PULPIT, AND PASTORATE

In the extraordinary popularity and rapidly-widening influence of his 'Fourfold State', as well as in the attractive power and abounding fruits of his ministry, Mr. Boston had now reached the central landmark in his life; and before proceeding further in narrating his biography, this seems to be the natural point at which to pause and introduce some more detailed statements in reference both to his home life and to the varied work which belonged to his sacred office.

In regard to his family, Mr. Boston showed an engrossing earnestness for the early conversion of his children. No doubt this zeal was intensified, and the burden of his responsibility became heavier, from the time that the mind of his beloved wife was shadowed by that mysterious cloud which was never removed but rather darkened, and she could no longer be his willing and happy helpmeet. It was his custom to pray regularly for his little ones, and also, in due time, to pray with them, as we find him recording: 'I had a particular concern this morning in my heart for grace to the young ones. I spake affectionately to my little Thomas about the state of his soul, and prayed with him.' He sought to have religious truths and Scripture stores interwoven with their earliest thoughts, all the more because he knew that these first memories and impressions seldom die out of the mind. He not only longed, but looked out, for the early dawn of the new life, assured that 'the flower when offered in the bud' was peculiarly welcome to him who had said, 'Suffer little children to come unto me, and forbid them not.' And he showed a similar concern for the supreme good of 'the man-servant and the maid-servant within his gates', recognizing the fact that they, too, were a part of his family for whose souls he was bound to watch. He wished to see in his manse at Ettrick 'a little spot enclosed by grace', and to have 'a church in his house.'

In this respect, as in so many others, the pastor of Ettrick stood side by side in spirit and practice with the pastor of Broad Oak and the other Puritan fathers of an earlier age. Particularly on the evenings of the Lord's Day, it was the unfailing practice of Philip Henry to gather his children around him, to pray with them, and to address questions to them, in their answers to which they declared their self-dedication to the three-one God. And then the saintly patriarch was accustomed to respond with loving solemnity, 'So say, and so do, and you are made for ever.' This beautiful story is told by Mr. Henry's own son, Matthew Henry, the great commentator, who had, no doubt, been one of the little band around the father's knees on whom the weekly benediction fell.

The transition is not difficult from Mr. Boston in his family to Mr. Boston in his closet. From the time of his youth, when we saw him kneeling beneath the branches of the apple-tree in the garden at Kennet, he found in secret prayer the congenial element in which his spirit lived, and moved, and had its being. And the morning and evening prayers were not sufficient to satisfy the cravings of his heart for prolonged intercourse with God, 'the living God'. In every condition he found an errand to the heavenly mercy-seat. For comfort in affliction, guidance in perplexity, help to repel temptation, strength for hourly duties and double strength for sacred work, he hastened with his empty vessel to the fountain of life; sometimes, when accusing himself of spiritual decay, or dreading the thought of divine desertion, 'wrestling for the blessing until the dawning of the day'. Like the young female convert in one of the South Sea Islands, whose chosen place of prayer was revealed by the beaten path that led to it, so might it have been said of this saintly man in connection with his solitary devotions. He was a man and a minister of the true Luther type, whom God makes 'strong to do exploits', and uses to revolutionise provinces and kingdoms. How much did Mr. Boston owe, for the wondrous success of his ministry and authorship in the highest forms of blessing, to this one holy habit, in which he laid hold of omnipotence! The same outward action would have been powerless and fruitless without this wrestling devotion, which said, 'I will not let thee go, except thou bless me.'

I wish to refer here more particularly to one practice which Mr. Boston, occasionally and at not very long intervals, joined with his secret devotions, and this was personal fasting, a conjunction of the two exercises familiar to us in the practice of the primitive church, and also in our Lord's teaching and references in his Sermon on the Mount and elsewhere, and the Book of Acts and the Epistles. We meet with allusions to it in various places in Mr. Boston's diary; and he even published in his later days an interesting little treatise in commendation of it, and for the guidance of those who had found it profitable for the soul at times to fast as well as to pray. We should, however, be seriously mistaken did we imagine that on such occasions when he mingled fasting with his devotions, there was anything of the nature of penance or afflicting of the body. To suppose this would be to lose the spirit in the body. He was no hermit. There was a partial, prolonged, or entire abstinence from food, and from bodily indulgences of every kind for a portion of the day.

But the supreme idea and aim of such fasting as our Ettrick pastor practised at times in conjunction with prayer, was the securing of absolute seclusion, the shutting out of all thoughts about the world and worldly occupations; and this for the purpose of self-examination, concentrating the mind upon the things which were unseen and eternal, and giving full opportunity for prayer to spread its wings and soar upward to heaven's gate. It was the soul 'panting after God', and guarding itself, as far as might be, against interruption or disturbance in its intercourse with the Father of spirits. It was the heart answering to the call of Jesus, 'Come ye yourselves apart into a desert place, and rest a while.' And sometimes, also, such holy seclusion was chosen by this servant of God when he had been smitten with some great affliction, or when he was called to the discharge of some peculiarly arduous and momentous duty. The fact that he continued this practice to the end of his life proves that he had derived conscious benefit from its observance. But one is apt to put the anxious question, How is it that this custom of godly men in an earlier age, or something kindred to it, is scarcely known among professing Christians in the present day? Has it not become as one of the lost arts? And therefore how many with a Christian name have become strangers to themselves! They have fallen into the perilous mistake of thinking that constant occupation with the business of the church, in its committees and week-day meetings, is, as a matter of course, an evidence of thriving religion; and in this way communion with their own hearts and with God is in danger of being jostled out. In the midst of over-engrossment and exaggerated activity they have ceased to hear 'the still small voice'.

We must now imagine ourselves to pass by a few steps from his closet into our pastor's study, where we see him seated at his desk with his open English Bible before him, and a Hebrew Bible and a Greek New Testament within easy reach, and his library, now of considerable size, surrounding him on every side. It has increased so slowly that he knows every volume, not only by its title-page, but by its contents. It would, however, be a mistake to imagine that the whole of his work in this apartment consisted in the preparation of discourses for preaching in that somewhat ancient church hard by, on the coming Sabbath. On the table there is a large manuscript volume, entitled 'Miscellanea', which bears the mark of much handling, in which he has written from time to time questions on difficult points in theology, some of which he has already succeeded in solving, while others are held in reserve; and on the other side there are several volumes of Hebrew learning, by the help of which he is elaborating theories regarding the accentuation of the Hebrew Scriptures for he leans to the opinion that the accents as well as the letters are inspired. But his principal work consists in the study of the Word of God, and especially in preparing the weekly 'tale of bread' for his beloved flock. This was not only a discharge of duty but a labour of love. He was in his element when he was in his pulpit, or when he was preparing for it. He so delighted in his message and in his Master, that he could have appropriated the language of holy Herbert, who was wont to speak of his pulpit as 'the preacher's joy and throne'.

We have seen that, in the earlier years of his ministry, Mr. Boston had frequent difficulty in fixing on a text for his sermons. Whole days were sometimes spent in an anxious and often an unsuccessful search; every part of Scripture seemed to him like a cabinet that was locked against him. And he felt this to be discouraging, even from a religious point of view. But, by degrees, these difficulties diminished and disappeared. Partly for this end, he began to deliver, at intervals, a series of expository and practical discourses on one verse or paragraph of Scripture. These sometimes occupied him for a long succession of Sabbaths; and it happened, not unfrequently, that when the passage had seemed at length to have become an exhausted mine, golden nuggets of saving truth continued to be brought to the surface by the pastor's holy ingenuity, to the wondering delight of his people. In addition to this, suitable texts and topics came to be suggested to him in his growing experience, sometimes by predominant sins in his parish, or by neglected duties such as family worship, or by events in providence such as a scanty or an abundant harvest, and, not least in value or acceptableness, by conversations with his people in his pastoral visits, or by his daily private and family readings of the Word of God. These at length became a *corps de réserve*, to which he could turn at any time in an emergency.

Like St. Augustine and St. Chrysostom – the latter of whom often drew down by his expositions of Scripture in the old cathedral at Antioch, the irrepressible plaudits of his delighted hearers – Mr. Boston had a strong liking for expository preaching;

and his gift went hand in hand with his preference. And often, when the whole discourse was not meant to be expository, he began with an exposition of the verse, in order to supply a solid basis for the doctrinal statements or practical admonitions that were to follow, according to Nehemiah's language, which admirably described so long ago what the exposition of Scripture should be – 'reading in the book of God distinctly, and giving the sense, and causing the people to understand the reading.' It was one of the maxims of our great Ettrick preacher, that 'all good preaching must be founded on good exposition'; that the function of the expositor is not to put his thoughts into the text, but to bring God's thoughts out of it.

And the instances were not few in which his introductory explanation of a verse which had seemed to his hearers, when announced by the preacher, obscure in its meaning and involved in its construction, became, in a little time, like the touching of a spring which let in heaven's light, or like the opening by the penitent woman of her 'box of ointment very precious', by which in a little time the whole apartment was filled with sweetest odours. I wonder what such a man as Boston must have thought of a preacher who, reading out as his theme for the hour some verse of Scripture which was full of Christ's love, or beamed with some 'exceeding great and precious promise', or was filled to the brim with consolatory words which were 'sweeter than honey, yea, than the honeycomb' immediately left it unheeded, or turned it into a peg on which to hang a disquisition on some secular subject, or by which to insinuate a half-veiled unbelief? Would he not have denounced the presumptuous trifler as guilty of profanity against Christ and of treachery and insult to his people who had come to him asking for bread and he had given them a stone or a serpent?

It may be affirmed with confidence that there was no minister in Scotland at that period of whom it could have been said with greater truth and fulness of meaning than of Mr. Boston, that he faithfully 'preached Christ'. I mean by this that he earnestly endeavoured to give to Christ in his preaching the same supreme and central place that he occupies in the Word of God. There we behold all the lines of inspired truth meeting in him, all the blessings of redemption provided by him and emanating from him. And it was the constant and commanding aim of this devoted and divinely-taught minister, to have his pulpit teaching conformed to this, alike in matter and spirit. We have only to look into his sermons in order to see to what a blessed extent his practice realized his aim. His whole teaching is fragrant as a garden of sweets with that 'name which is above every name'. We find him dilating with holy delight on the various parts of Christ's redemption work on which the salvation of the human race depended, and tracing it in its various stages from the one eternity to the other: Christ who 'was in the beginning with God, and was God', coming forth, in the fulness of time, from the bosom of the Father, and becoming incarnated in our humanity, in order that he might be qualified for working out our salvation in all its glorious and benignant issues; – Christ in his perfect obedience to the divine law, and in his atoning sufferings and death as the substitute of sinners, enduring in their behalf the penalty of sin, and 'bringing in an everlasting righteousness'; – Christ in his triumphant resurrection from the dead, receiving the Father's public testimony to his approval and acceptance of his atoning work, and 'powerfully demonstrated to be the Son of God'; – Christ ascending to heaven, taking possession of its many mansions in his people's behalf, there making continual intercession for them, and receiving from his Father's hand the sovereignty of the universe, 'all power being given to him in heaven and on earth', in order that by the dispensation of the Holy Spirit and the administration of his providence, he might in due time bring his innumerable redeemed to glory.

With kindred gladness do we behold him, as an ambassador of Christ, making free offer to the whole fallen race of man of all the blessings which have been provided by Christ's redemption work, free as the air we breathe or as the light of day, and the actual bestowal of these, in all their divine and immeasurable riches, 'without money and without price', upon every child of man who should take him at his word and believe in his name. And how often do we find the preacher's language tasked and strained to the utmost, to admeasure and to understand, when he proceeds to speak of those redemption blessings which meet all men's necessities as sinners and all their capacities as creatures – the full and irrevocable forgiveness of sins; reinstatement in the divine favour and friendship; the gift of the Holy Spirit in his enlightening, purifying, and peace-giving influences, turning men into living temples of the living God; victory in death and over death; the reception of the ransomed soul at death into the Father's house, into the fellowship of the angels and the beatific vision of God; the resurrection of the body at the end of the world, made like unto the glorified body of Christ, and united for ever to the glorified spirit; triumphant acquittal at the last judgment, and ascension with Christ and all his redeemed to the heaven of heavens, where 'they shall for ever be with the Lord'.

These were the themes of transcendent interest which enriched and glorified the preaching of Mr. Boston, and which made it so mighty a power for the highest good, so that, at the period of which we are now writing, there was scarcely a cottage home in all Ettrick that did not contain some of his converts, to whom he could have said, 'What is our hope, or joy, or crown of rejoicing? Are not even ye in the presence of our Lord Jesus Christ at his coming?' To a large extent Ettrick, in this second decade of his ministry, had been transformed into a garden of God.

And beyond all this, Mr. Boston felt that if he was to preach Christ faithfully and fully, it was indispensable that he should present and explain the moral law to his hearers, not only in its outward letter, but in its spirituality and comprehensiveness, and also in its evangelical sanctions and motives. Was not Christ Prophet and King in his church; and must not those who claimed to be his followers be instructed in the knowledge of the King's laws? To do this was included in Mr. Boston's commission as a Christian minister, and, in its own time and place, was to preach Christ.

And beyond the matter of his sermons, there were characteristic qualities in the style and imagery in which they were clothed, which were fitted both to arrest and to retain the attention of his hearers. It was not often that he was chargeable with unnecessary divisions and subdivisions which were apt to perplex the understanding and to overtask the memory of his hearers. In general, his thoughts were arranged in a succession of paragraphs which presented a connected and continuous train of instruction. And these were expressed with simplicity and beauty, and with an unfailing freshness which did not remind you of the lamp, but rather of the newly-plucked flower from the garden, with the morning dew upon it. These paragraphs again were often wound up with a compact sentence which was proverbial in its point and brevity, and seemed to gather into itself the whole essence of the passage. So that even now, when the whole sermon is read in its unity, it is apt to remind us of one of the Ettrick hills, smooth and green to the summit, with here and there a daisy or a wild violet refreshing the eye with its modest beauty.

Another prominent and engaging feature in much of Mr. Boston's preaching consisted in the frequency and felicity with which he drew his illustrative imagery from the natural scenery of Ettrick and the social customs of its people. This, when skilfully done, was eminently fitted both to win the attention and to assist the understanding and the memories of his hearers; and the practice has been adopted in every age by some of the greatest and most successful preachers. It is one way of bringing home the truth to the business and bosoms of men. How often did the divine Teacher himself use the scenery and customs of Palestine to be the garment and vehicle of his matchless and priceless lessons, and emphatically in his parables, which have made the world richer for all time. The sower going forth to sow, the tares mingled with the wheat, the shepherd going out to search for his lost sheep, the woman searching for her lost piece of silver, the fishermen drawing their net and separating the precious from the worthless – these and many more of his everyday surroundings were employed by the heaven-sent Teacher to make the entrance of his lessons into the hearts of men the more easy, and to secure that, once there, they could never be forgotten, and so to make the earthly do service to the heavenly.

It has been remarked that after the Civil War, in one of whose regiments Jeremy Taylor served for a time as chaplain, his sermons drew much of their colouring and imagery from the camp and the battlefield. It was similar with the minister of Ettrick. There were few of his sermons that did not, in some form of other, reflect and reveal his outward surroundings, and turn them to holy uses. The changes in the seasons, the aspects of the sky, the sudden thunder awakening the echoes of the everlasting hills, the sheep knowing the shepherd's voice, the bemisted traveller unable to find his way, the sheep buried in the snow, the shelter of the sheepfold, the market and the fair with their bargainings and contentions – these and many outward things were used by him as garments to enrobe spiritual truth or to point a moral lesson, and, as it were, made 'to pay tithes to the ministry'.

We are led to conclude from some incidental hints, that in the earlier periods of his ministry Mr. Boston had fastidiously abstained, even after long intervals, from preaching sermons to his people which he had formerly addressed to them. Whether his reason for this was the groundless fear that he might be suspected of indolence by such an indulgence, or an unwillingness to act thus in the face of an unreasonable prejudice on the part of some of his hearers, it would not be easy to determine. But as he advanced in years, he became less scrupulous, especially when his health was impaired and study had become for the time a weariness, and he allowed his people to taste some of 'the old wine'. And he was encouraged in this somewhat rare indulgence when, on a certain sacramental occasion, he first preached a newly-written sermon, and at a later hour of the same day an old sermon selected from his large bundle of manuscripts, and he found that the latter was the more appreciated of the two by his hearers. 'That,' says he, 'was it which the Lord made the most sweet to the people and to me.' It did not occur to the tenderly scrupulous minister that in preaching the same sermon from his Ettrick pulpit, after a considerable interval of years, he was really not preaching to his old congregation, and that by a large proportion of his listeners it was heard for the first time. Besides, he had sanction for such judicious repetition in the words of an apostle, when he well knew that the cause was not indolence or self-indulgence, but the need of relief from an excess of mental toil and strain, lest the bow being too long bent should break; for 'to write the same things unto you, to me indeed is not grievous, but for you it is safe.' Moreover, a sermon when so repeated after a considerable lapse of years, is likely to gather into it new thoughts derived from new experiences. The language of Mr. Fuller on this subject is marked by his wonted wit and wisdom, and was probably meant, not only as a suggestion to others, but as a vindication of his own practice. These are his words:

> 'As for our minister, he preferreth rather to entertain his people with wholesome cold meat which was on the table before, than with that which is hot from the spit, raw and half-roasted. Yet in repetition of the same sermon, every edition hath a new addition, if not a new matter, of new affections. "Of which," saith St. Paul, *we have told you often*, and now we tell you weeping."'

We have yet to look at Mr. Boston in the pulpit. It was often noticed by his family and others that he always lingered long in his study on the morning of the Lord's day; and they well knew the reason. He was preaching his sermon to his own heart before he went forth to preach it to his people; and he was wrestling hard in earnest and continuous supplication for that almighty help without which even the preaching of the true evangel was impotent.

We know of only two ministers in Scotland at that period whose preaching was equally owned and honoured of God with Mr. Boston's and these were Ralph and Ebenezer Erskine, whose names occupy an honoured place in Scottish Church history; and whose sermons are still to be seen in stately folios in the libraries of our older ministers, and, dressed in the garb of the Dutch language, in many of the rustic homes and congregational libraries of Holland.

His natural gifts as a preacher must not be left by us unnoticed. In his countenance there was the mingled expression of majesty and benignity; and this, when lighted up by the kindling emotions produced by the sacred themes on which he spoke, attracted and retained the attention of his hearers. And his fine musical voice, which had been trained in his youth, increased the effect of his speaking, and made it pleasant for the crowding multitudes to listen; while the rare and beautiful figures in which he often clothed his thoughts and emotions added another charm to his oratory.

But all these qualities and gifts, so valuable in their own place, would have failed in the great and paramount end of the Christian ministry had they been alone. The message of the gospel in some of its many grand aspects must be the theme of the preacher, and his own heart must be in sympathy with it, if he is to be the instrument of winning souls into the kingdom of God. The eloquent preacher without the gospel may attract multitudes, but his eloquence alone will never save a soul. But in the union of these two qualities in his weekly ministry, we have the secret of Mr. Boston's great success. In those happy days of which we are writing, there was scarcely a Sabbath in which he did not receive the welcome tidings of some instance of the highest form of blessing in the conversion of hearers. Scarcely did the gospel net ever come up empty. The people hung upon the preacher's lips. So rapt was the attention that every sound was hushed into silence but that one pleading voice. There was not only influence but fascination. How different was all this from Mr. Boston's experience at the beginning of his ministry in Ettrick, when he was often hindered in his preaching by many of his people walking out, without reason or excuse, while he was speaking; giving utterance to all manner of uncouth sounds, and to loud conversation and laughter afterwards around the church door. But in these later times a change had come which was not of earth. And all Ettrick owned its benignant power. Had one followed the people to their homes, after those holy services which we have been describing, he would have found them, ere long, breaking up into little companies for conversation on the sermons to which they had listened and of which their hearts were full, and helping each other's memories for the better storing up of the lessons of the day. And then they would find that the 'heads' and 'particulars' into which the earnest preacher had arranged his instructions had not been without their uses, but had been as hooks by which the better to recover and retain what they had heard.

There was one remarkable incident which repeatedly occurred in connection with Mr. Boston's preaching, and which revealed much in regard to his pulpit influence and power. At the sacramental services in those times, which, as we have seen, drew many thousands together and extended over the greater part of the sacred day, it was common and even necessary to have many ministers engaged, who should preach in rotation, the one after the other. Of course, Mr. Boston had his full share assigned to him in these services. But, again and again, after he had preached, the minister whose turn it was to succeed him in the pulpit refused to ascend and occupy his empty place. And when he was asked to state his reason for this unwonted course, his answer was that the impression made by Mr. Boston's sermon had been so great, that he was afraid and unwilling to follow him, lest he should unwittingly undo the blessing.

I must refer in this connection to the extent to which Mr. Boston's incessant labours as a pastor contributed to the power and influence of his preaching. Those words of Paul to the elders of Ephesus, so full of holy wisdom and melting tenderness, every sentence touching a chord in their bosoms, might have been spoken by the minister of Ettrick to his parishioners, though his reference embraced in it a much longer ministry: 'I have shewed you, and have taught you publicly, and from house to house. I ceased not to warn you night and day with tears.' It is when we see these two parts of his ministry combined and co-operating, preaching and pastoral visitation, and all of course conjoined with prayer, that we can the more easily account for that rich harvest of souls which he was again and again called upon to reap. Those tears of sympathy watered the good seed of the word which he had sown. Those home visits, winning their affections and their confidence, invested his preaching with a double power, and opened the way for the entrance of the word. 'The sheep knew their shepherd's voice,' and followed him. As we have seen, it had been the same 'in measure' at

Simprin. They could not doubt the reality and strength of his love. And with what grief and even anguish did he receive the unwelcome intelligence of flagrant sin in the case of any in the flock. Such wounds struck very deep. With what sympathy also did he hear of the sickness, or bereavement, or crushing disappointment of any of his members, and, making their trials his own, hasten to their homes, however far off. 'Who was weak, and he was not weak? Who was offended, and he burned not?' That pastor's heart was the chosen depository of his people's sorrows, and cares, and joys. And he knew the special value of personal interviews with individuals in his parish who had come into circumstances of peculiar moral danger or difficulty, calling for counsel, or stimulus, or warning. The youth who was rising to manhood undecided and without experience, was always an object of his special interest, whom he would invite to his manse, and warning him against surrounding temptations and perils, urge him to immediate decision for Christ. Nor was the backslider left unwarned by him, but entreated not to lose his first love; and the instances were not few in which those of his flock who had begun to wander from the fold were brought back with thanksgiving and prayers and tears.

When his congregation saw him enter his pulpit on the morning of the Lord's Day, they knew that they were looking into the countenance of one who had just come forth from intimate communion with God, and who was at once God's ambassador and their friend. Along with his devout and holy living, he united in himself two great influences – his preaching and his pastoral oversight, in which he 'watched for souls as one that must give an account'. But the minister who holds himself back from the latter of these functions, when it is within his power to use it, is like a man that is content to work with only one arm. So long as his health continued unbroken, Mr. Boston delighted in this part of his sacred office, ready to face storm and rain and cold in visiting the dying and the disconsolate, even to the remotest parts of his parish; and it was only when advancing years came, bringing with them decaying health and growing infirmities, that he reluctantly obeyed their unwelcome interdict to hold back.

'Wide was his parish, not contracted
In streets, but here and there a straggling house;
Yet still he was at hand without regret
To serve the sick, or succour the distrest,
Tempting on foot alone, without affright,
The danger of a dark tempestuous night.'

8

HEBREW STUDIES AND
FOREIGN CORRESPONDENCE

It has already been mentioned that, in addition to his regular studies in his weekly preparations for his pulpit, there were two special subjects of study to which Mr. Boston was accustomed frequently to turn aside, not only as a pleasant diversity for study, but for self-improvement and the enrichment of his ministry. The origin of one of these is easily accounted for. It happened not unfrequently, especially in his early years at Simprin, that in the course of his usual studies for his Sabbath teachings, questions would arise which perplexed as well as interested him at the moment – theological problems which were new to him, but which required more of thought and reading and prayer satisfactorily to answer, than he could give to them at the moment. These he did not cast aside, but took careful note of them, that he might turn to them with avidity and concentrated mental energy when an opportunity for prolonged meditation offered itself. In a large volume, which he called his 'Miscellanea', he stated the subject in the form of queries, leaving an ample number of blank pages for recording the answer when the knot of difficulty had been untied, and for stating the reasonings by which his conclusions had been reached.

We give the following examples of his queries: 'Where hath sin its lodging-place in the regenerate? Why the Lord suffereth sin to remain in the regenerate?' It is not difficult to understand how questions like these must have multiplied in the hands of the earnest student in those earlier years of his ministry, and how the 'Miscellanea' did not long remain a blank book, especially when we remember that, in his young ministry, he did not possess a single commentary on the Bible, and his other books, which lay on his few half-furnished shelves, might have been counted and catalogued in a few minutes. This, however, as we have seen, was not all disadvantage, for the lack of books threw him back the more upon his personal resources, and accustomed him to independent thinking; and the prize of knowledge, when it was won by him after this fashion, was doubly precious. We may imagine him, many years afterwards in Ettrick, turning over those difficulties in earnest devout thought in his long walks in its glens or upon its hillsides, and also in his meditations during the night watches. The queries, with the answers, were not published in Mr. Boston's lifetime; but they were edited, at some interval after his death, by his son, when he had become a minister in Jedburgh.

The answers to the two queries which we have named cover together thirty closely-printed pages. The reasoning is masterly, ingenious, and fresh as newly-plucked flowers. And it is pleasant, while we read, to trace his footsteps into light, and to feel that one theological problem more had been set to rest. We quote the closing paragraph in his elaborate answer to the question, 'Why the Lord suffers sin to remain in the regenerate?' 'Finally, to shut up all, it is plain that the more difficulties the work of man's salvation is carried through, the free grace of God is the more exalted – our Lord Jesus, the author of eternal salvation, hath the greater glory. But in this way it is carried on over the belly of more difficulties than it would have been if, by the first grace, the Christian had been made perfect. And seeing none can prize rest so much as they who have sore toiled, and have come out of the greatest tribulations, I think I may be allowed to say that a child of God, having come to his journey's end, after so many ups and downs, falls and risings, having won through the troublesome sea of this world, and being set safe ashore after so many dangers of shipwreck in a longsome voyage, will have the praises of free grace in his mouth sounding more loudly, and will sing the song of Moses and the Lamb in a more elevated strain and higher notes, than if he had never been in danger through the whole of his course. From all which it appears that this dispensation is most suitable to the grand design of the gospel, exalting the riches of true free grace in Christ. And what lover of Christ will not say, Amen?'

Another subject of study which eagerly engaged Mr. Boston's thoughts alongside of his weekly preparations for his pulpit, was the Hebrew Bible, with the grammar and structure of the Hebrew language. It has already been mentioned that a copy of the Old Testament in its original tongue came early into his hands, in his young and happy days at Simprin; and almost from the beginning he became deeply interested in it; and all through his ministerial life it continued to be the almost daily pasture-ground of his intellect and heart. It was like a fountain which had been suddenly opened at his feet, and which flowed on alongside of his daily path. The fact that the Hebrew Bible was written in the very language in which God had communicated with men through patriarchs, and kings, and prophets in the earlier revelation, and in which the moral law had been conveyed by the hands of Moses from the summits of the thunder-riven Sinai, gave to it, in his estimate, a peculiar and sacred fascination. We find him in his diary and letters, calling the Hebrew the 'holy tongue', and speaking of it as his 'darling study'.

It was natural that he should begin his systematic reading of the Hebrew Scriptures with the Book of Genesis, and he was not slow to acknowledge that he was amply awarded from the first by the new light which it flashed upon many a sentence in the English version, the Hebrew vocables being in many instances 'word pictures'. These discoveries made him happier for the day, and were laid up by him in store for future use. In his riper ministry he seldom preached from a text in the Old Testament, without previously examining the Hebrew original, making it contribute to the freshness and fulness of his instructions.

It was not many years after he had begun the systematic study of the Hebrew Scriptures that Cross's 'Tagmical Art' came into his hands; and the book with its novelty of thought introduced a new subject of inquiry and element of interest into this branch of sacred learning. One prominent topic was the accents in the Hebrew text, which had usually been regarded as helps to the pronunciation of the words and nothing more, and as fitted to produce a pleasant uniformity in this respect. But the author of the 'Tagmical Art' contended for the divine original and authority of those accents – that they were as old as the words of the Bible, given also by divine inspiration, and had to do not only with the sound but with the sense of the Scriptures.

Mr. Boston was greatly interested by this theory, and, from the beginning, regarded it with favour; not only because of the ingenuity and plausibility of some of its arguments, but also because he persuaded himself that if it could be satisfactorily established, it would both add to the contents and value of the Bible, and shed welcome light upon not a few passages whose meaning was now dark or doubtful. We find him writing to Sir Richard Ellys, an accomplished English scholar, and a devout man, in such glowing and sanguine terms as the following: 'Through the divine favour falling on the scent, I was carried into the belief of the divine original and authority of that accentuation as stigmatological, seeing glaring evidence of the same in my reading of the sacred Hebrew text, shining by means thereof in its own intrinsic light.' Again: 'A happy explication or genuine representation of the nature of the accentuation of the Hebrew Bible, in its natural and artless contrivance, is the only thing wanting to procure it the same awful regard with the other parts of the sacred text.'

His enthusiasm on this subject brought him into correspondence with some of the most distinguished Biblical scholars on the European continent, many of whom regarded the discussion not only with interest but with favour, sincerely hoping that the evidence might be so convincing as to warrant their taking their place on the side of the Scottish divine. Among those friendly onlookers and inquirers were such eminent Dutch scholars as Schultens and Gronovius at Leyden, and Loftus at Rotterdam. The better to facilitate intellectual intercourse and a comparison of views, Mr. Boston not only wrote an essay of considerable length on the divine origin and authority of the accents, but translated it into Latin, which in those days was the common language of learned divines; in this way the better securing against his being misunderstood, and widening the interest by largely increasing the number of readers. The solid learning of the Scottish minister, writing from amid the obscurity of his Scottish mountains, and the ingenuity of his reasonings, along with his modesty and outshining piety, charmed his readers and prepossessed them in favour of his views; while the great issues in connection with the interpretation of Scripture which they anticipated, if he should succeed in justifying his convictions on the divine inspiration of the accents, made them wish for his success. There were many friendly onlookers candid in their doubts, but pausing for the weight that would turn the scale.

One of his most attached and scholarly friends writes to him in these encouraging words: 'If your essay on the Hebrew accentuation succeeds, it is a glorious work. Has Providence directed you to rules for ascertaining the sense of Scripture, or at least for reducing it in some good measure to a greater certainty than heretofore? For my own part, I had rather be the author of such a book than master of the Indies. The very failing in an attempt of this nature has its merit. "*Magnis tamen excidit ausis*," you know is given as no mean character.'

It is an interesting fact that, at some time during Mr. Boston's correspondence with those foreign theologians, his 'Fourfold State', which had already borne a new life into myriads of homes in the southern and eastern counties of Scotland, had found its way among the divines and pastors of Germany and Holland, and through them among the people. It is not improbable that copies may have been sent, in the first instance, by the author himself. At all events, we have the testimony of letters written to him that it was read by many with lively interest and permanent benefit. The free and full-orbed gospel which it presented as the message of heaven's love to every human being, and the warmth and pleading earnestness with which it was conveyed, unlike the cold and philosophic stateliness which was too much the characteristic of modern books of divinity in those days, made readers feel that they were brought into contact with matters, not of mere speculation or dialectic discussion, but of supreme personal interest to themselves. Holy earnestness pulsed in every sentence, and those who read could not remain indifferent. It was acknowledged by many, with glowing gratitude, that Mr. Boston's 'Fourfold State' had introduced them to clearer views of the great central doctrines of saving truth, and made plainer to them the way of life. His precious life-book met a great and clamant necessity. God loved them, and so loved them as to give his only begotten Son for their redemption. It did for multitudes in those foreign lands in theological schools and in the homes of the common people, what his own reading of the 'Marrow' had done so long ago in the soldier's cottage at Simprin for himself.

In the course of time, as was natural, the correspondence between the good Ettrick pastor and those Continental scholars slackened and ultimately ceased, partly because of his impaired health, and his occupation with engrossing controversies and ecclesiastical troubles, which had begun to show themselves at home.

Meanwhile, in passing from this subject, it may be remarked that had Mr. Boston been acquainted with facts which came into notice at a somewhat later period, he would not have committed himself with so much confidence and enthusiasm to the opinion that the accents formed part of the Old Testament revelation from the beginning, were given by divine inspiration along with the other parts of the Hebrew text, possessed equal authority, and formed part of the Old Testament canon when it was completed. But scholars by-and-by arose who hesitated, and at length found themselves shut up by increasing knowledge to the denial of the inspiration of the Hebrew accents. They argued, that if those accents formed an essential part of the text of the Hebrew Scriptures from the beginning, how was it that in looking into the writings of the early Christian fathers, such as Jerome, Origen, and others, in many of which they quote profusely from the Hebrew Bible, those accents are uniformly absent and unknown? There seemed only one answer to this question – namely, that they did not then exist. Another fact is equally significant and conclusive, that the copies of the Hebrew Scripture which are read in the Jewish synagogues are the oldest in the world, and their completeness and purity have all along been guarded with the utmost veneration and jealousy, even to the minutest jot or tittle; and in these again we look in vain for the accents.

The most probable account of their origin and uses has been given by the Jews themselves, who, speaking by the Rabbi Elias Sevita, ascribe the invention of the accents to the doctors of Tiberias in the fifth century of the Christian era; and this judgment has been confirmed by the most learned Rabbins. They further inform us that these accents were never meant to take their place as a part of the Hebrew text, but to give direction and uniformity in the pronunciation of the words. They were mere human aids introduced for convenience, which meddled in no degree with the sense but with the sound of the words which had been given by inspiration of God. We may be certain that more than one of these facts were unknown to this saintly man; and that, if he had known them, he would not have spoken and written in assertion of the antiquity and inspiration of the accents, with the confidence and persistent zeal which marked his conversation and correspondence on the subject. The thought of an addition being virtually made to the text of the Old Testament Scriptures, and new facilities being discovered for interpreting their meaning, dazzled his imagination, and almost made him wish to live longer that he might help in bringing the untold treasures to light. He and those of his learned contemporaries who thought along with him were like men working in a mine of gold, who imagined that they had come upon a new vein which would immeasurably add to their riches. It was a fond imagination which appealed to some of their most sacred instincts, and it died hard. But the consensus of later generations has gone against it, and at length it has passed away, 'like the baseless fabric of a vision'.

9

GATHERING CLOUDS

In Mr. Boston's own parish of Ettrick, peace and religious prosperity had long reigned. It was like a carefully watched and well cultivated garden, and the affection and reverence of the people had increased with their pastor's years. But when he looked forth beyond the circuit of those green hills, there were not wanting signs and incidents to awaken his anxiety and alarm.

Defection in doctrine, creeping like a leprous taint, was becoming in various forms more aggravated and pronounced in the teaching of positive and perilous error. In 1717, Professor Simson, the lecturer in theology in the university of Glasgow, was charged at the bar of the General Assembly with the teaching of several unscriptural tenets which savoured of Pelagianism; and although the charge was proved, the censure of the Assembly amounted only to a gentle hint 'to be careful of his language'. About the same time, Professor Campbell, of the sister university of St. Andrews, when it was shown that he had vented errors of an even darker hue, was treated with a similar unfaithful daintiness.

Mr. Boston was not slow to predict, at the time, that such inadequate discipline on the part of those who were the appointed guardians of the church's faith and purity, instead of deterring, was likely to encourage to bolder heresies. And his words were prophecies. For, after the lapse of several years, it was found that by that time Professor Simson had so far diverged from 'the faith

127

once delivered unto the saints' as even to have called in question, in his lectures to his students, the supreme divinity of our Lord Jesus Christ, the foundation truth of Christianity as well as of Christian hope; and instead of dismissing the betrayer of his sacred trust from his office and deposing him from his ministry, as the majority of presbyteries in the church had recommended to be done, the General Assembly satisfied itself with suspending him, in the meantime, from the discharge of his ecclesiastical functions, which left him to enjoy all the emoluments of his office. The supreme gravity of these dealings consisted in the fact that the men who were treated with such guilty leniency were the persons to whom had been entrusted the training of the future ministers of the church; and that a censure so utterly inadequate on the part of the rulers revealed a widespread indifference to Christian truths even the most vital, or a secret sympathy with what had been so timidly condemned. The wound was filmed over with plaster when the surgeon's amputating knife was needed. Let us at once follow this part of the story to its end.

On this momentous occasion, which tried men's hearts, there was only one man who had courage enough to stand up and utter his solemn and indignant protest against this action of the Assembly; and this solitary man, reminding us of Athanasius of old in the Council of Nicea, was Thomas Boston of Ettrick. Rising with a solemn majesty that became him, and inspired with that fear of God which delivers from every other fear, he entered his dissent in the following words which made many around him quail: 'I cannot help thinking, Moderator, that the cause of Jesus Christ, as to the great and essential point of his supreme deity, is at the bar of the Assembly requiring justice; and as I am shortly to answer at his bar for all that I say or do, I cannot give my assent to the decision of this act. On the contrary, I find myself obliged to offer a protest against it. And therefore, in my own name, and in the name of all that shall adhere to me, and, if none here will, for myself alone, I crave leave to enter my dissent against the decision of this act.'

Timidity rather than treachery or indifference, a desire to maintain an outward semblance of peace, and perhaps also a fear to incur the displeasure of those ecclesiastical rulers who sat there in their 'pride of place', must be held as explaining the unworthy silence of many of Mr. Boston's brethren on this occasion, who held themselves aloof from him when they should have been found standing at his side, sharing the responsibility of his protest, and ready, at all hazards, to put honour upon him whose 'name was above every name'. They lost a grand opportunity of testifying their fidelity to him who had promised to those who confessed him before men, that 'he would confess them before his Father and his angels'. And, no doubt, their conscience was not long in telling them this, when it arose in their bosoms like an armed man. It is recorded that their recollection of this scene, and of their failure in duty in the testing hour, haunted the death-beds of many of those brethren, and though it did not extinguish their hope, it disturbed their peace. In an epitaph on Mr. Boston, written by Ralph Erskine, his faithful friend and fellow-witness for the truth, reference is made to this heroic act, when he seemed to stand alone 'faithful found among the faithless':

'The great, the grave, judicious Boston's gone,
Who once, like Athanasius bold, stood firm alone;
Whose golden pen to future times will bear
His name, till in the clouds his Lord appear.'

Years before this event, the heart of Mr. Boston had also begun to be grieved and filled with anxious forebodings, because of the negative style of preaching which was becoming fashionable in many of the pulpits of the Scottish Church, especially among its younger ministers. I mean by this, that while none of the great truths of our religion were directly denied or even questioned by those ministers, they were held back, and something else was substituted in their place which did not contain that vitalizing power by which God converts men and brings them within the kingdom of the saved. They preferred to linger in the outer court of the temple, and seldom turned their gaze to the inner shrine in which the glory dwelt. They did not regard the divine injunction, 'first to make the tree good, and then the fruit would be good'. They were strangers to the divine method of creating men anew, which was to begin with the heart, and then to work out from it upon the whole circumference of the outward life. Moral precepts were coldly stated, not unfrequently in elegant sentences; but nothing was said of those evangelical motives which win and bind the heart to Christ, and which, constraining to a loving service, make his yoke 'easy and his burden light'. They seemed to be more concerned about the beauty of the vessel than about the nutritious qualities of the food contained in it. That secret power which, under the preaching of such earnest men as Knox, and Henderson, and Rutherford, had roused multitudes to repentance and kindled within them a new life, was not there; their 'drowsy tinklings lulled their flocks to sleep', and the people went home empty and unblest, to indulge their former worldliness, perhaps to hug their old sins.

There was another mode of preaching not unknown in those days, which, though it did not aim to destroy the gospel, tended to mutilate it, to mar its power, and to dim its glory, the thought of which had many a time made the heart of our earnest pastor sad, as he sat and mused in his mountain home. I refer to those who denied the free, unlimited offer of Christ in the gospel to mankind sinners as such, and asserted that this 'deed of gift and grant' was made to the elect alone, or to such as had previous qualifications commending them above others. What a barrier of discouragement and repulsion did this place around the fountain of life! The gospel in the teaching of such men was like the glorious sun under dark eclipse. Who among the fallen sons of men could know by this whether he was invited to the feast of heaven's love or not? How different from that gospel, 'in its full round of rays complete', which Mr. Boston and those who were like-minded with him rejoiced to proclaim, that 'Jesus Christ was God the Father's deed of gift and grant to the whole human race.' There was no exception in its message; and in sending it to the world, it proved and proclaimed that God loved the world. It invited every human being to its warm embrace. If I were travelling alone in an African desert, and met one poor naked savage, I would have warrant to assure him, on the authority of God's own word, that there was a gospel for him. At the very period of his life of which we are now writing, and after seventeen years' experience in holding forth this word of life to his fellow-men, we find Mr. Boston writing thus: 'The warrant to receive Christ is common to all. Though I had a voice like a trumpet that would reach to the corners of the earth, I think I would be bound by my commission to lift up my voice and say, "Unto you O men, I call, and my voice is to the sons of men." None are excluded but those who exclude themselves. But the convert of yesterday is the young heir of glory.'

And another kind of teaching, in some respects kindred to this, and with which the gospel message was grievously hampered, was connected with the name of Principal Haddow of St. Andrews, who was soon to come into unenviable prominence in connection with approaching ecclesiastical conflicts. He insisted on the necessity of a certain amount of moral preparation on the part of the sinner, for receiving the gospel and entering on the possession of its priceless benefits. The gospel, as he taught it, did not all at once say, 'Come', but 'Wait' until you are more deeply humbled, and have undergone a certain amount of outward preparation. This was rightly described by Mr. Boston as a 'gilded deceit', and a 'trick of the enemy of souls' to keep the man back until those temporary impressions had faded away; while, in the case of others, it tended to generate a self-righteous spirit, as if the man were coming with a price in his hand and trying to do for himself what Christ was waiting to do for him. To quote the pointed words of Riccaltoun, 'Such preachers would have persons whole before they come to the physician, and clean before they come to the fountain.'

At that same period, the efficiency of the pulpit for its supreme ends was greatly marred, in the case of not a few ministers, by their inadequate and misleading views of what has been fitly termed 'the gospel method of sanctification'. Their strain of preaching produced the impression that the attainment of a certain measure of outward morality might realize at length what was meant by sanctification, and lift men up to that state of heart and character which this great word in our Bible theology describes. But the clear and uniform teaching of Scripture is that, in every instance, the first indispensable step towards sanctification consists in the man's being brought into friendly relations with God – in other words, in his 'justification through faith in the righteousness of Christ imputed to him.' The moment that this blessed change takes place in him, he becomes united to Christ, and is made a partaker of the renewing influences of his Holy Spirit; and this justifying faith produces and sustains in him that love to God in Christ which is the root and germ of all true holiness in the heart and life. And this evangelical holiness cannot be produced in any other way. There may be outward morality and seemly acts of kindness without it, but holy love reigning in the heart, and working out in holy service on the whole circumference of the outward man, so as to make it evident that he has been created anew, and that the image of Christ is reflected in him, must be preceded by, and can only come through, justification. 'As the branch cannot bear fruit of itself, except it abide in the vine; no more can ye, except ye abide in me.' It was a favourite and characteristic saying of Boston, 'Let them that *will*, repent, that Christ may do for them. I believe what Christ hath done for me, that I may repent.' There cannot be any acceptable obedience where there is no love, and there cannot be love where there is no faith. The same thought was beautifully expressed in a later age by one who, like Mr. Boston himself, was a native of Duns: 'The tear of repentance is shed by the eye of faith; and faith, as it weeps, stands beneath the cross.'

> Talk they of morals,
> O thou bleeding Lamb, thou teacher of new morals to mankind;
> The grand morality is love of thee.'

It is indeed the judgment of many, that in describing the gospel method of sanctification, even more than that of justification, Mr. Boston and the two Erskines and the other Marrowmen did the greatest service to sound theology in their days; and perhaps some modern preachers who are, in the main, evangelical, but do not yet fully comprehend 'the perfect law of liberty', would do well to clear their mental vision with eye-salve gathered from the discourses of those 'masters in Israel'.

The Neonomian doctrine imported from England, which, though not asserting, like Antinomianism, that, under Christianity, the believer was not subject to the divine law as a rule of life, yet taught that the standard of the law was lowered in order to accommodate itself and make it more attractive to human frailty, began to be whispered at times from certain Scottish pulpits, and in some of Mr. Boston's later sermons we can see this faithful watchman's hand lifted up in protest and warning against its insidious and plausible teachings.

But there was, no doubt, a bright side to this picture, and this consisted, not least, in the body of divinely enlightened and earnest ministers of Christ to which Mr. Boston belonged, and in the eager multitudes who flocked to their ministry. And beyond the Boston circle, the number of ministers and congregations was still not few who held fast in all its purity and fulness 'the faith once delivered unto the saints', and adorned their Christian profession by their holy lives. But those many-coloured signs of divergence from 'the form of sound words', and those numerous instances in which, while error was not taught from the pulpits, saving truth was withheld and there was a corresponding decay of spiritual life among the people, were such as to alarm and sadden the hearts of those men of God who placed the cause and kingdom of Christ upon the earth supreme in importance above all other interests. Had the question been put at this period to our Ettrick pastor, 'Watchman, what of the night?' he would probably have answered in such terms as the following, which we gather from his diary and letters: 'The stream of gospel doctrine, which sometime was clear, is now disturbed.' 'Truth is fallen in the streets.' 'Zion's wounds are multiplied in the house of her friends.' 'The song of the watchman is marred.' We might imagine him, as he wandered in such moods of mind, far from the haunts of men, in one of the glens of his own Ettrick, to have sung in plaintive notes these words of the psalm –

'By Babel's streams we sat and wept,
When Sion we thought on.
In midst thereof we hanged our harps
The willow-trees upon.'

A state of things had now been reached in the condition of the
Scottish Church which brought men together who remained true
to the old gospel of the Reformation and whose bodies were the
temples of the Holy Ghost, that they might confer and pray together
as to what should be done in such a grave emergency. Boston's
own 'Fourfold State' was passing into the hands of ministers and
people, and was soon to work like a heavenly leaven and with
unabated power and ever-widening sphere in many parts of the
land. But in addition to this, it was now resolved by those
assembled fathers and brethren to secure the republication and
extensive circulation of the 'Marrow of Modern Divinity'; a book
which, as we have already seen, mainly consisted of the best
thoughts of the best men on the great truths of evangelical theology
– great reformers, renowned authors, eminent preachers, professors
in universities, in many lands and through many generations – the
primary stars of their age. We have found that this remarkable
book had been greatly blessed to Mr. Boston in his early ministry,
and to others among those fathers and brethren who were now
sitting with him in devout and anxious consultation, having given
to them, as it were, a second spiritual birth. It seemed to these
venerable men that such a measure as had been proposed was
eminently fitted to counteract those evil tendencies which were
showing themselves in so many forms in many parts of Scotland.
It was a God-given thought and purpose, as the issue abundantly
proved; though, as we are now to see, the carrying of it into effect
was for a time most bitterly and unscrupulously opposed. We are
now briefly to relate the story of the publication of the 'Marrow'
in Scotland.

10

THE 'MARROW' CONTROVERSY

Early in 1719, the Rev. James Hog, minister of Carnock, a man of singular intellectual gifts, and described by his contemporaries as one of the holiest ministers in the kingdom, republished the first part of the 'Marrow of Modern Divinity', with a preface strongly recommending it, in which he dwelt on its seasonableness as meeting contemporary errors in reference to the all-embracing nature of the gospel message and the true way of obtaining gospel holiness. In the beginning of April, in the same year, Principal Haddow of St. Andrews University preached a sermon before the Synod of Fife, in which he especially attacked the 'Marrow'. This sermon was immediately printed and published at the desire of the synod. Soon after, he published another sermon, which bore the reckless and misleading title of 'The Antinomomianism of the "Marrow" detected'. In both of these the 'Marrow' is charged with containing and vindicating such revolting positions as these: 'Holiness not necessary to salvation'; 'The believer not under the law as a rule of life'; 'Rewards and punishments no motives to obedience'. And all this is written and charged against a book, the second part of which is devoted to a masterly exposition of the ten commandments!

Both these productions were promptly answered, and the unblushing ignorance revealed in many places exposed, by the dauntless friends of a full-orbed gospel. In all these early contendings, an onlooker might have seen the gathering clouds which portend the storm.

The men who were sitting in the high places of power in the church, and not a few of whom were unfriendly to evangelical truth, were indignant at and hostile to this action of the friends of the 'Marrow'. And they were not slow in giving form to their hostility. The General Assembly of 1720, founding on the report of a committee which had been appointed to 'inquire into the publishing and spreading of books and pamphlets', not only condemned the 'Marrow', but prohibited its ministers from either preaching, writing, printing, or circulating anything in its favour; further enjoining them to warn their congregations against its perusal. Here was the Index Expurgatorius in the supreme court of the Scottish Church. 'It is understood,' said Mr. Boston, 'that Principal Haddow was the spring of that black Act of Assembly.' Could a book abounding in blasphemy, or proclaiming infidelity, or apologizing for licentiousness, have been more severely condemned? And yet there were thousands in the parishes of Scotland at that very time who had been sitting under a sapless ministry, and who had found this very 'Marrow', when it came into their hands, to be like heavenly dew or hidden manna to their fainting and famished spirits. 'I would not,' said one, 'for ten thousand worlds, have been a Yea to the passing of that Act.' Many of the best ministers and private members of the church were astounded and grieved. And at the General Assembly of the following year, Ebenezer Erskine and eleven other ministers, among whom was Mr. Boston, laid upon its table a document, afterwards known in Church History as 'The Representation', remonstrating against the condemnation and interdict, as an unwarranted restraint upon their liberty; a rejection, in some instances, of doctrines which were precious in themselves, and which they believed to have full warranty of Scripture; and a wounding of Christ in the house of his friends. It was written with fearless candour, but in a respectful and conciliatory spirit; while there was a ready admission of the existence of defects in the 'Marrow', with all its excellence, making it evident in every page that the aim of its compilers was not the gaining of a controversial victory, but the conserving of truths which were more precious to them than life.

But there was no returning to wiser courses. On the contrary, 'The Representation' was not only condemned, but its twelve supporters, who had come by this time to be known as *the Marrowmen*, were ordered to be rebuked at the bar of the Assembly. They have been justly spoken of as 'the truest ecclesiastical patriots of their times'. The names of several of them stand honourably prominent in church history, and in the theological literature of their age. And the names of all of them are surrounded to this day by a sweet fragrance in the parishes in which they laboured, through the double ministry of their preaching and their lives. They are as follows –

	Minister of the Gospel at
James Hog	Carnock
Thomas Boston	Ettrick
John Bonar	Torphichen
John Williamson	Inveresk and Musselburgh
James Kid	Queensferry
Gabriel Wilson	Maxton
Ebenezer Erskine	Portmoak
Ralph Erskine	Dunfermline
James Wardlaw	Dunfermline
Henry Davidson	Galashiels
James Bathgate	Orwell
William Hunter	Lilliesleaf

With calm dignity and holy gravity, those faithful confessors stood forward and endured the censure, 'rejoicing that they were counted worthy to suffer shame for the name of Christ'. In his diary, Mr. Boston has this record: 'I received the rebuke and admonition as an ornament put upon me for the cause of truth.' 'It is better,' said another of those faithful witnesses, 'to be under the reproach of men for following Christ, than to be under the curse of God for forsaking him.' It must, however, be remembered that, while only twelve ministers appeared at the bar of the Assembly in this supremely important cause, they were only the leaders in the conflict, and there remained many others who preached the same doctrines of the Reformation, and were the hearty friends of the Marrowmen.

Their action and endurance on that eventful day were not yet completed. For immediately after 'giving in' their united and solemn protest against the Act which had condemned the 'Marrow', they declared that it should be lawful for them to preach and bear testimony to the truths contained in it. But in high-handed violation of the constitutional rule for protecting the consciences of minorities, the protest was refused to be recorded, and the further indignity was added of not allowing it to be read in the Assembly. Rights were in this way wrested from their hands, which had been bought and sealed by the blood of martyrs.

One is apt to wonder that while those ecclesiastics were sending forth their condemnation of the 'Marrow', and fulminating their interdicts against those ministers who had promoted its republication and circulation, it had never occurred to them that if the 'Marrow' was a book of such dangerous tendencies as they had never wearied in pronouncing it to be – a thing not safe to be 'touched, or tasted, or handled' – then the authors of the book were surely more severely to be blamed than those who had taken part in its circulation. But mark now where the stroke of the anathema falls. The 'Marrow', as we have already seen, was not the production of one mind, but mainly consisted of brief extracts, sometimes individual sentences, from the writings of eminent authors who were the friends of evangelical truths, from the Reformation downwards. The book was a miscellany of choice sayings and select passages from the works of the greatest authors of their times, stretching back through many ages. Great reformers and eminent scholars and theologians, such as Luther and Calvin, and Knox and Beza, and others who, in their day, had formed 'the flower and chivalry' of the Puritans, are made to unite their mental stores in illustrating 'the faith once delivered to the saints.' And one great fact stands out with peculiar interest, that the 'Marrow' was one of the books specially recommended by the famous Westminster Assembly of Divines in 1643. How shall we account for the fact that the same book which was specially commended by that august assembly, the compilers of the 'Confession of Faith' and the 'Catechisms Larger and Shorter', the greatest thinkers and most profound theologians of their age, should have been branded with interdict and anathema by the General Assembly of the Scottish Church in 1720?

But all these keenly persistent efforts against the 'Marrow' and the Marrowmen were unavailing. The people who were forbidden, at their peril, even to read the 'Marrow', would not consent to walk blindfold, or to be led whithersoever their ecclesiastical rulers listed. They were determined to judge for themselves, 'proving all things, and holding fast that which was good'. The 'Marrow' was accordingly purchased and eagerly read, during those years of controversy, by thousands over the land, with the effect of conversion in the case of multitudes, and of increased knowledge, holiness, and joy in the case of others who had already believed. It was to many of them like passing from dim twilight into gladdening sunshine. They now, for the first time, saw 'the glorious gospel of the blessed God' in its 'height and depth, and breadth and length'. Mr. Boston himself tells us that it turned to the great advantage of many, both among ministers and people, being obliged both to think of these things and 'to inquire into them more closely and nicely than they had done before'. And referring in another place to the 'Marrow' controversy, this is his record: 'That struggle, through the mercy of God, turned to the advantage of truth in our church both among the ministers and the people; insomuch, as it has been owned, that few public differences have had such good effects, and saving truths have, in our day, been set in an uncommon light.' He seemed to himself to witness, in the case of many, the repetition of his own experience in 'sweet Simprin' so long ago, when he saw the gospel illuminated and enlarged with a new splendour, and it appeared to him, to quote his own words, 'like a chariot paved with love'. The sight of happy converts rejoicing in their new life was immeasurably more than a compensation to him for all the humiliation and the evil treatment of the last three years.

And the blessed influence of this remarkable book was found, within the next quarter of a century, to have spread beyond Scotland, and to have proved a benefit to preachers and authors whose reputation, in those years, filled the mouths of men. George Whitfield, whom we might almost style the evangelist of two hemispheres, acknowledged with enthusiasm the good he had derived in his ministry, both in England and America, from the study of the 'Marrow'.

And Mr. Hervey, the distinguished author of 'Theron and Aspasio', a book which in those days might have been seen in almost every Christian home in England, wrote thus in the year 1755: 'I never read the "Marrow" with Mr. Boston's notes till this present time. I find that by not having read it I have sustained a considerable loss. It is a most valuable book. The doctrines it contains are the life of my soul and the joy of my heart. Might my tongue and my pen be made instrumental to recommend and illustrate, to support and propagate, such precious truths, I should bless the day wherein I was born. Mr. Boston's notes on the "Marrow" are, in my opinion, some of the most judicious and valuable that ever were penned.' Of two outstanding doctrines of the 'Marrow', – the free grant of Christ to sinners as such, and the special application of the faith of the gospel, – Mr. Hervey also says: 'These two doctrines seem to me the very quintessence of grace and the riches of the gospel. They are, I am certain, the sovereign consolation of my soul; at least they are the channel and conveyance of all comfort to my heart.'

It would not be difficult to trace the influence of this remarkable book upon creeds and testimonies, as well as upon religious thought and Christian experience, in days much nearer to our own. It tinctures the phraseology of our religious literature and conversation, and shapes our thoughts, without our knowing from whence the influence comes; just as it is possible for us to drink from a stream, and be refreshed by its waters, without our being aware of the fountain from which it has flowed far up among the everlasting hills.

11

THE LAST DECADE

We are now some years, in our narrative, within the last decade of Mr. Boston's life. It is eight years since his beloved wife was smitten with that insanity which brought her mind under dark eclipse, and shadowed the formerly bright and happy home at Ettrick. That fine spirit, so full of love and tenderness, and lighted up with wisdom, had become like a defaced and ruined temple. Her husband touchingly speaks of her as, during those past years, having been as 'the slain that lie in the grave, and are remembered no more'. And he goes to say that, 'being overwhelmed with bodily maladies, her spirit dried up with terror by means of her imagination in a particular point, and harassed with Satan's temptations plied against her at that disadvantage.'

We learn, however, that there came at times lucid intervals, in which 'the Lord had given her remarkable visits in her prison, and manifested his love to her soul'. And it seemed as if the soul-music had come back again to the old Ettrick home, 'proving that the reality of grace was in her, and could not be quenched'. She even said, 'Who knoweth but that the Lord will bring us again to the land of the living?' And her husband had welcomed the gleam of hope, as the weary traveller through the long midnight welcomes the dawn. 'Now,' says he, 'we were with our broken ship within sight of the shore, and I was like one stretching out his hand and crying, Help forward, help forward. But, behold, a little time after, the storm rose anew, and the ship was beaten back into the main ocean, out of sight of land again.' But, continuing 'to hope against hope', we find the meek and enduring sufferer writing thus, at a later period, of his wife and himself: 'I was helped to believe that we would both stand on the shore yet and sing, notwithstanding our swelling seas.' The hope was to be exceeded a hundredfold in a heavenly sense ere many years had run their course.

So early as 1719, Mr. Boston's strength had begun to show symptoms of decay. The afternoon of his life had begun, with its lengthening shadows. But he would not allow this to hinder, or even to slacken his activity as a preacher or an author. The effect was rather, in the meanwhile, to quicken it, for he knew that his time was short. About the close of the 'Marrow' controversy, he had sent forth, at the request of his brethren, a volume of 'Notes on the Marrow'. This he soon after joined in one volume with the 'Marrow' itself, which greatly added to the interest and usefulness of both. We have seen in what glowing terms eminent authors standing in the front ranks of theologians and writers on Christian experience, like Mr. Hervey, the author of 'Theron and Aspasio', spoke of the benefit, both in knowledge and in spiritual impulse, they had derived from the Notes of the Ettrick pastor.

In 1721 and 1722, he delivered an elaborate series of discourses to his Ettrick flock on the two Covenants – the Covenant of Works and the Covenant of Grace. They show much of the learning and manner of Witsius,[1] while they excel him in freshness and fervour. The people must have been fond of strong meat who relished and hungered after such sermons. But if they demanded thought, they richly rewarded it. The two courses formed an elaborate system of evangelical theology, and were admirably adapted to meet and expose the rising errors of the times, such as Antinomianism with its license to sin, while giving many a 'root-stroke' to crude thoughts which were the growth of half knowledge. The motto of

---

1. Herman Witsius (1636–1708) was a Dutch divine who wrote on the Covenants. Christian Focus Publications, Ltd., Tain, Ross-shire, also publish *An Analysis of Herman Witsius' 'The Economy of the Covenants'*, Beeke & Ramsey, ISBN 0908067223, Mentor, Tain, Scotland, 2003.

the book, as sounding the keynote of the whole treatise, might have been given in the words of Paul: 'As in Adam all die, even so in Christ shall all be made alive.' It was not published until after Mr. Boston's death.

Following the preaching of those elaborate and exhaustive discourses on the two covenants, Mr. Boston soon after delivered a series of sermons on Christian morals, their general designation being 'Sermons on the distinguishing characters of true believers'; and associated with these and with kindred aims was a little group of sermons on Philippians 2:7 – 'Christ's taking upon him the form of a servant.' These were characterized by his brethren at the time as 'masterly'. Our Ettrick pastor seems to have been followed in this action by his brethren of the 'Marrow' generally. And, no doubt, this was done primarily for the purpose of instructing their people in practical religion, both by showing the meaning and comprehensiveness of the moral law, and stating the Christian motives by which obedience to it was prompted and sustained in the believer in Christ. But another reason was, by expounding and enforcing in their teaching the moral law, to deliver the minds of multitudes from the impression which had been produced by the Act of Assembly, which charged the 'Marrow' and the Marrowmen with the loathsome Antinomian error that the believer in Christ was not under the law as a rule of life – an Act which had never, up to that hour, been repealed. Mr. Boston justified the course that had been taken by himself and his brethren by remarking that the gospel doctrine had got a wound by that Act which condemned the 'Marrow', and which charged it with containing doctrines which every Marrowman not only rejected and condemned, but loathed from the very depths of his heart. Why should it have 'lien among the pots' so long? Bring it forth to the light, that men may see that its 'wings were of silver and its feathers as yellow as gold'.

Somewhat later in the decade, Mr. Boston preached to his people a series of sermons on Affliction. These were subsequently published under the memorable title of 'The Crook in the Lot', being mainly founded on the text in Ecclesiastes 7:13 – 'Consider the work of the Lord: for who can make that straight, which he hath made crooked?' The sub-title is given in a more expanded form, and is like the bud opening into the blooming flower: 'The sovereignty and wisdom of God in the afflictions of men, together with a Christian deportment under them.' The foundation truths in the passage are stated by himself to be the following: 1. That whatever crook there is in any one's lot, it is of God's making. 2. That whatever God sees meet to mar, no one will be able to mend, in his lot. 3. That the considering of the crook in the lot as the work of God – that is, of his making – is the proper means to bring one to a Christian deportment under it. These, with the truths and lessons which grow out of them, are stated and illustrated with a vigour and a pathos, and enriched with a fulness and variety of Scripture fact and incident, not to speak of that proverbial point in many of his sentences which we have seen to be characteristic of all his best writings, as to have made it, next to the 'Fourfold State', the most popular of all Mr. Boston's works. While written by him in decaying health, the book proves that his intellectual strength was undiminished. There is a freshness in almost every page which reminds one of the dew-laden grass upon the green hills of Ettrick. How many a sorrowing heart, from those days onwards down through the ages, has drunk consolation from 'The Crook in the Lot', and found the bitter waters of Marah turned into sweetness. To how many has it proved in God's hand a sanctifying power, drawing from them the wondering and adoring acknowledgement, –

'Among the choicest of my mercies here
Stand this the foremost, that my heart has bled:
For all I bless Thee; most for the severe.'

The proverbial maxims are specially valuable, as they are also specially memorable. Let us gather and bind together a few flowers and fruits from this part of Mr. Boston's garden:

1. 'God makes none of his people to excel in a gift but, some one time or other, he will afford them use for the whole compass of it.'

2. 'When God wills one thing and the creature the contrary, it is easy to see which will must be done. When the omnipotent arm holds, in vain does the creature draw.'

3. 'There are many prayers not to be answered till we come to the other world, and there all will be answered at once.'

4. 'There is never a crook God makes in our lot but it is in effect heaven's offer of a blessed exchange to us. Sell whatsoever thou hast, and thou shalt have treasure in heaven.'

5. 'Impatience under the crook lays an overweight on the burden, and makes us less able to bear it.'

6. 'A proud heart will make a cross to itself, where a lowly one would find none.'

7. 'It is far more needful to have our spirits humbled and brought down than to have the cross removed.'

8. 'It is a shame for us not to be humbled by such wants as attend us; it is like a beggar strutting in his rags.'

9. 'All men must certainly bow or break under the mighty hand.'

10. 'Lay your account with it, that if ye would get where the Forerunner is, ye must go thither as he went.'

11. 'Who would not be pleased to walk through the dark valley, treading in Christ's steps?'

12. 'Standing on the shore, and looking back on what you have passed through, you will be made to say "He hath done all things well." Those things which are bitter to Christians in passing through them, are very sweet in the reflection on them. So is Samson's riddle verified in their experience.'

13. 'Let patience have her perfect work. The husbandman waits for the return of his seed, the sea-merchant for the return of his ships, the storemaster for what he calls ear-time, when he draws in the produce of his flocks. All these have long patience. And why should not the Christian too have patience, and patiently wait for the time appointed for his lifting up?'

12

HOME IN SIGHT

In the beginning of the last year of his life, which we have now reached in our narrative, Mr. Boston published a treatise of no great bulk, but which came up to his wonted mark of excellence, and proved that, however much his bodily strength might have been impaired, it would, in the freshness of its style and the vigour of its thought, as in the case of 'The Crook in the Lot', have been worthy of his middle life. The book was entitled 'A Memorial concerning Personal and Family Fasting and Humiliation'.

These personal fasts, as we have seen, had been practised by him during the whole period of his long ministry, and he believed that they were clearly warranted in many places both in the gospels and the epistles; nor is he slow to testify in his booklet that he had derived invaluable religious benefit from them during his long Simprin and Ettrick life. We shall here introduce a few of his valuable thoughts which have not been anticipated in our former references to the subject. He takes good care to indicate that there was nothing of penance or will-worship in the fasting which he commended and practised. He explains that religious fasts thus kept in secret 'by a person apart by himself, are not the stated and ordinary duties of all times to be performed daily, or at set times recurring, such as prayer and praise and reading of the Word are; but that they are extraordinary duties of some times to be performed occasionally, as depending entirely, in respect of the exercise of them, on the call of Providence, which is variable.'

We must imagine the individual fencing off a day, or part of a day, in which he shall have withdrawn from intercourse with others and from the common avocations of life; and in some private apartment where he has secured himself against interruption, and sought to be alone with God, he shall give himself up entirely to spiritual exercises. It may be that, during this period, there shall be entire fasting or abstinence from food, or that the taking of food shall be only diminished in degree. In this and kindred matters every one must be a law to himself. What is best to be done in these circumstantial matters must be regulated by Christian prudence, and determined by the individual for himself. It must be remembered that things like these are only as the shell to the nutriment contained in it.

In stating the various parts of religious exercise which are comprehended under the head of personal, and equally of family fasting, Mr. Boston mentions the following; it being understood that prayer is an element which shall pervade and animate the whole like the sunlight, in which the solitary worshipper shall live and move and have his being, while it shall come into special prominence in some parts of the exercise:

1. There must be self-examination, or 'consideration of his ways', on the part of the Christian seeking to discover what is wrong or wanting in his manner of life, in order that he may humble himself before God because of it.

2. Free and full confession before God of his sins, especially of those which have been discovered and brought out to light from their hiding-place, in order to his seeking deliverance at once from their guilt and their power. 'See if there be any wicked way in me, and lead me in the way everlasting.'

3. Exercises of repentance towards God with special reference to those sins, in order to his returning from them to God in heart and life. And it may well be that the penitent in his solitariness name those particular sins, and dwell upon them in their humbling aggravations. 'If we are indeed true penitents, we will turn from

sin, not only because it is dangerous and destructive to us, but because it is offensive to God, dishonours his Son, grieves his Spirit, transgresseth his law, and defaceth his image; and we shall cast away all our transgressions, not only as one would cast away a live coal out of his bosom for that it burns him, but as one would cast away a loathsome and filthy thing for that it defiles him.'

4. Extraordinary and prolonged prayer as the humble and self-accusing utterance of this repentance, and also with special reference to that which had been the immediate occasion of the fast.

5. Entering anew into covenant with God by taking hold anew of his covenant of grace through believing in the name of Christ, whereby we take hold of the covenant and are instated in it unto salvation; in mentioning which Mr. Boston remarks, with well-timed tenderness that 'one may take hold of God's covenant of grace, even though it be with a trembling hand.'

We close our reference to Mr. Boston's treatise on fasting, by quoting two sentences which are worthy of being treasured in the memory of those who are willing to be his disciples:

'Lay no weight on the quantity of your prayers – that is to say, how long or how many they are. These things avail nothing with God, by whom prayers are not numbered but weighed.'

'The laying over of a matter on the Lord, believingly in prayer, gives great ease to a burdened heart; it turns a fast sometimes into a spiritual feast.'

Mr. Boston was made conscious by increasing signs that 'the sands of time were sinking'. In addition to the feeling of diminishing strength, there were frequent attacks of 'gravel', producing acute pain and accompanied by 'paralytical shakings of the head'. In all this, Nature was holding out signals of distress, the meaning of which could not be misunderstood. It led him, among other things, to make arrangements with a view to the disposal of his worldly goods after his death, especially in making provision for his children and assigning them equal portions. This was promptly done, not only to prevent those embittering family feuds which are the frequent result when this part of parental duty is neglected, but, as he himself expressed it, with the design 'to have no remembrance about worldly affairs when the Lord should be pleased to call him home'. And with what sad and thoughtful tenderness did he also made adequate provision for that loved one sitting in the gloom of her 'inner prison', in the event of her being left behind him, cherishing the while the assured hope that ere long they would meet again in that world where

> 'The quenched lamps of hope are all relighted,
> And the golden links of love are reunited.'

And there was another matter which, at this time, pressed itself on the anxious thoughts of the good Ettrick pastor, attention to which came within the scope of the divine command to 'set his house in order'. He had good grounds for believing that three out of his four children were already true disciples of Christ. But there was still one, the youngest, just budding into manhood, about whose religious condition he was uncertain and anxious. 'Oh that Ishmael might live before thee.' The youth was sent for at once by his saintly father, and the object of his errand affectionately declared. A few prayerful and loving interviews assured Mr. Boston that his youngest son was 'not only almost, but altogether persuaded to be a Christian'. To use the father's own favourite language, he believed that 'Jesus Christ was God's deed of gift and grant to mankind sinners, and therefore to him'. This was Christ's gospel. He accepted it, and the gift became his. The words of the hymn written in a later century reflected the thoughts of the happy parent as he grasped the hand of the young communicant, his youngest son:

> 'When soon or late we reach that shore,
> O'er life's rough ocean driven,
> We shall rejoice no wanderer lost,
> A family in heaven.'

A few weeks after, Mr. Boston, when administering his last communion, with grateful and gladdened heart that brought tears of joy to his eyes, saw this son of his many prayers and vows sitting at the Lord's Table amid the numerous band of young confessors of Christ.

At an advanced period in those waning months, Mr. Boston 'renewed his covenant with God', in order, as he expresses it, to his preparation for death. On repeated occasions, at earlier periods, as we have seen, he had, after the review of his life and confession of sin, declared his renewed acceptance of God's covenant of grace. And with some changes in the language, indicating his more enlarged views of 'the glorious gospel of the blessed God', the solemn transaction was now repeated, as if in sight of the eternal world. He described himself, as on those earlier occasions, 'after a period of prolonged prayer, rising from his knees, and while he stood alone in his chambers, lifting up his eyes to the Lord, reading before him the acceptance he had written, and subscribing it with his hand.' We shall quote his own detailed account of this last renewal of his covenant with God:

'Rising early in the morning, after my ordinary devotions, I spread the subscribed acceptance of the covenant before the Lord, and I solemnly adhered to it and renewed it. Then proceeding towards the covenant, I stated God's offer and exhibition of it to me in his own express words; – such as Isaiah 55:3: "I will make an everlasting covenant with you, even the sure mercies of David." This is the covenant, Hebrews 8:10: "I will put my laws into their mind, and write them in their hearts: and I will be to them a God, and they shall be to me a people. For I will be merciful to their unrighteousness, and their sins and their iniquities will I remember no more." Hosea 2:19: "I will betroth thee unto me for ever." John 3:16: "God so loved the world, that he gave his only begotten Son, that whosoever believeth in him should not perish, but have everlasting life." Revelation 22:17: "Whosoever will, let him take the water of life freely." These,' continues the devout man, coming out from the presence chamber of his covenant God – 'these I pleaded were his own words, he could not deny it; and thereupon I adhered and solemnly took hold of the same as before. And then I saw so clearly the matter concluded between God and my soul, that I could plead and see that, upon the separation of my soul from my body, my soul should be carried up by angels into Abraham's bosom, by virtue of the covenant; and my dead body be carried down to the grave in it, and lie there in it, and, by virtue of it, raised up at the last day reunited to my soul. And tongue and heart jointly consented that this my vile body, bearing the image of the first Adam, should be left lifeless, carried to the grave, and become more loathsome there, till it be reduced to dust again; but so that, in virtue of the covenant, it be out of the same dust new framed and fashioned after the image of the second Adam, like unto his own glorious body. Rising up from prayer with joy in believing, I sang with an exulting heart Psalm 16:5 to the end, –

"God is of mine inheritance
And cup the portion;
The lot that fallen is to me
Thou dost maintain alone.

"Unto me happily the lines
In pleasance places fell;
Yea, the inheritance I got
In beauty doth excel."

It was about this time that Mr. Boston received welcome intelligence regarding the acceptance and usefulness of his 'Fourfold State' in remote places, and particularly in the Highlands of Scotland. And not long after, his heart was cheered by his receiving kindly notice of the publication of a new edition of his precious treatise, a copy of which was not long in finding its way to Ettrick. The manner of his reference to this in his dairy is truly characteristic of the man of God. 'I took it,' he says, 'and spread it before the Lord, praying for a blessing to be entailed on it, for the correction and conversion of sinners and the edifying of saints, for the time I am in life, and after I shall be in the dust.' Little did the modest author venture to indulge the fond imagination that, within little more than thirty years, the book would have passed through more than thirty editions, some of them very large. It would have seemed to him like a presumptuous dream; but it was exceeded by the fact. Who can compute the spiritual results within the same period?

There was another event in this closing period of his life which was surrounded with a peculiar and sacred interest, in connection with the observance of the Lord's Supper by Mr. Boston and his people in the midsummer of 1731. For it was anticipated by the beloved pastor, with his growing infirmities, that this would be the last time in which he would dispense among them this 'heart-strengthening ordinance'; and the same thought, though yet unspoken, was in the minds of his people. What hallowed memories and melting associations stood connected with the thought of former communions, in which the language of their hearts had often been, 'Surely it is good for us to be here'. But this approaching sacrament was to bring with it associations and impressions peculiarly its own. The good pastor, as he gazed forth upon those deeply-impressed multitudes with his look of mingled majesty and benignity, could have said to them, in the language of the Master, 'I shall not drink henceforth of this fruit of the vine, until that day when I drink it new with you in my Father's kingdom'. All Ettrick was moved by the anticipation. The parishioners came forth on that occasion in numbers that had never before been equalled. Even the lame, and the halt, and the blind would not consent to be absent. From 'lone St. Mary's Loch' to the gates of Selkirk, from the picturesque glens of Yarrow, and places far beyond, they hastened, streaming from the early morning dawn; throwing themselves with confidence upon the unfailing hospitality of their Ettrick brethren, some of whom provided lodging for fifty strangers, while others were equally lavish in providing meat and drink. This, as we have already stated, was one of the last things which Mr. Boston noticed in his diary. And he did it with holy gladness and gratitude. 'God,' says he, 'hath given this people a largeness of heart to communicate of their substance on these and other occasions also. And my heart has long been on that occasion particularly concerned for a blessing on their substance, with such a natural emotion as if they had been begotten of my body.'

The communicants were strangely moved as they heard their pastor's solemn and tender voice repeating the 'words of institution', and received from his pale and trembling hands the sacred emblems of the Redeemer's dying love, and thought that this was the last time in which he would preside at the holy festival. Still, the joy on that occasion swallowed up the sorrow. The records left behind regarding it lead us to think of it as a day ever to be remembered, a little Pentecost, a foretaste of the time when all the emblems shall have vanished away, and Christ shall be seen by his people face to face.

We here introduce two letters which were written to Mr. Boston at this period by two of his brethren in the ministry, whose names are already familiar to us, as belonging to the innermost circle of his friends – Gabriel Wilson of Maxton, and Henry Davidson of Galashiels. Their ointment and perfume, no doubt, 'rejoiced his heart', on the way to his heavenly home.

Letter from Mr. Wilson.

Rev. Dearest Brother, –
It has been a most real pain to me, after I was fully purposed to be with you some time this day, to think of sending any letter. But the ordering seems to be of the Lord. I design to essay it again without delay, according as I hear from you. I hear the trial has become still more fiery; but hope you will be kept from thinking it strange, as though some strange thing had happened unto you. Oh, it is difficult; but you are allowed, and even called to rejoice, inasmuch as you are thus made 'a partaker of Christ's sufferings'.

The Lord has in great favour led you forth into his truth, and is now in his fatherly wisdom giving you use for it all – calling you to show forth the supporting and comforting power of it. Our season, if need be, of being in heaviness through manifold temptations is made up of hours and minutes, and will soon run out (2 Cor. 4:17, 18).

The Son of God, your Lord and Master, is with you in the furnace, though not always visible, and will never leave you nor forsake you. May the God of hope, of patience, and consolation, 'the God and Father of our Lord Jesus Christ', 'the Father of mercies', and 'the God of all comfort', comfort you in all your tribulation with the comforts of his covenant, and with the same comforts with which he has enabled you to comfort others in any trouble. You mind (Ps. 31, *ult.*) that it is in the way of our labouring to be of good courage that he promises to strengthen our hearts. I will still hope and seek that he may turn the shadow of death into the morning, and spare you to recover strength.

Our Session being met this day, in token of their love and sympathy have sent the bearer, one of their number, to visit you and bring them word. Dearest brother, I desire to remember your bonds, as bound with you. Great grace be upon you. – I am, with love to all yours, dearest Sir, yours,

Gab. Wilson.

Maxton, April 8, 1732.

From Mr. Davidson.

Very Dear Sir, –

Your several letters came safe to hand, and were very acceptable. This comes to inform you that the good old woman, my mother, went home to her own, the better country, this morning, betwixt three and four o'clock. She took her bed upon the Lord's-day evening; had a fever pretty high, but retained all her senses to her dying hour. How cruel is our love! How blind and inconsiderate is our affection! We would prefer the small advantages of greater gains we reap from their abode with us, to entire satisfaction and complete happiness – a very great but common solecism in true friendship we are often guilty of. However frightful and ill-favoured death may appear to the eye of sense, it is viewed by faith as the messenger of our heavenly Father; and when the Christian opens its hard cold hands and looks into them, there are to be found gracious letters full of love, bearing an invitation to come home, a call from the new Jerusalem to come up and see. When death with the one hand covers our eyes, and deprives us of the light of the stars with the other, it rends in pieces the veil, and so makes way for our being set immediately under the refreshing beams of the Sun of Righteousness, without the least appearance of a cloud through the long ages of eternity. Now that 'his way is in the sea, and his path in the deep waters, and his footsteps are not known', we believe loving-kindness in all the mysterious passages of Providence; we shall in due time see 'a wheel in the wheel', and be taught how to decipher the dark characters; we shall, with an agreeable surprise, perceive an all-wise Providence, in all its intricate, oblique, and seemingly contrary motions, to have been a faithful servant to the divine promise, so that we may say Amen to heaven's disposals, and cry out in the dark and gloomy night, Hallelujah. I should certainly make an apology for giving you so much trouble, but allow it to be written to the Lord's prisoner of hope with you, as I design it, though the direction bears your name. The fault of its length will, I hope, appear less when taken in that view. My affectionate respects to Mrs. Boston with yourself, are offered by him who is, very dear Sir, yours very affectionately in the straitest bonds,

H. Davidson.

Galashiels, February 25, 1732.

Meanwhile Mr. Boston's strength was gradually diminishing; and this was aggravated, as well as his pain greatly increased, by a scorbutic disease which had fastened upon him as a permanent malady. This made it necessary, however reluctantly, that he should begin to lessen his pastoral labours, though he could have said of the unwelcome change, with another devoted servant of Christ and lover of souls who had become old in the ministry, 'Oh, it is hard for me to give up working in the cause of such a Master.' For instance, up to this advanced period, it had been his unvarying practice, as will be remembered, to hold 'catechizings' in the homes of his people, once in the year, over the whole of his parish. Neither inclement weather, nor swollen stream, nor steep and rugged mountain path could hold him back from this part of his pastorate, which he had valued and enjoyed as bringing him into close contact with the minds and hearts of his people, keeping up his acquaintance with their family history, and, not least, enabling him to gauge the measure and accuracy of their knowledge in the verities of the gospel of Christ. But this must now be abandoned as having not only become a difficult but an impossible service.

And yet the loved work of catechetical teaching was not, wholly and at once, given up. There was a sort of compromise with difficulty. The devoted minister clung with enthusiasm to his favourite service. When he was no longer able to meet with parents and other adults in their homes and remote districts, it was arranged that the younger people should come from all parts of the parish, at stated times in the week, to meet with Mr. Boston in the kirk; and a portable iron grate was provided by the kind people, in which a peat fire was kindled on the appointed day, beside which the earnest minister of Christ, with sixty or seventy young men and women gathered around him, could address them during an hour that never was wearisome while he conversed with them of the great things of God.

But the interval was probably not very long until another change was needed. For the frail and palsied state of his limbs made it irksome and even impossible for him to stand in his pulpit while preaching; and his sympathizing people, knowing of what all these signs were the prophecy, were glad to prolong his ministry among them, were it even for a little time, by placing a large arm-chair in the Ettrick pulpit, in which he could sit and discourse. The voice to which so many of them had listened from their infancy no longer possessed its earlier strength and power, but its wonted tenderness and pathos were still there; and every Sabbath they listened with the saddened feeling, which made every sentence the more precious, that these might be his last words. They knew that they were now gathering the gleanings of the vintage. Ere long the cry of their hearts would be,

'Oh for the touch of a vanished hand,
And the sound of a voice that is still!'

Even this thoughtful arrangement served only for a time; for at length, because of his growing frailty, Mr. Boston could no longer venture outside of his manse to preach, and his last expedient was to preach from one of the open windows of the manse to large and loving congregations stretching away before him, with the sublime background of the everlasting hills. Two excellent sermons on the necessity of self-examination (2 Cor. 13:5) were written by him for these occasions, and preached from this extemporized pulpit.

Two things may be gathered from Mr. Boston's sayings during those later months of his life. One of these was that those grand evangelical truths, which it had been the special work of his ministry to preach and to defend, were the support of his mind at the last, when he knew, by many symptoms, that the end was near. Referring to that favourite sentence, more 'precious than gold, yea, than much fine gold', 'This is the record, that God hath given to us eternal life, and this life is in his Son' (1 John 5:11), which contained the condensed spirit of the Marrow divinity, we have found him saying, when looking back upon a period of dangerous illness, 'This was the sweet and comfortable prop of my soul'. And on another occasion, when stricken down with a sudden illness, and in the immediate prospect of death, he leaves this testimony of his experience: 'The grant of Christ to sinners, as such, was the ground of my comfort; and since Saturday last, I have had experience of the solid peace and joy of believing God to be my God.'

And the other noticeable circumstance was, that he had no desire to outlive his activity and usefulness. His desire rather was, that when he ceased to work he might cease to live. This feeling shines out in such sayings as the following: 'I have some comfortable prospects of the weary's getting to rest'; 'I had some special concern on my spirit this day, for being helped to die to the glory of God, that when death comes I might be ripe and content to go away.' If he had been asked, during his closing weeks, to say whether he had any unsatisfied wish, the spirit of his answer would have been in the words of the dying Melancthon, 'Nihil aliud nisi coelum' (Nothing else but heaven). And the end, when it came, was in welcome harmony with his desire.

Mr. Boston's mental attitude was now one of waiting expectancy for his summons to his heavenly home, like Elijah looking up for the descending chariot of fire. So much was this the case, that he promptly discouraged every form of interruption that threatened to disturb his equanimity, and to draw his thoughts back to 'the things which were seen and temporal', which he had left behind him for ever. This appears from his answer to a correspondent in Edinburgh, who, unaware of his condition, had written to him on some matter of secular business. The letter is interesting, not only because of the state of mind which it reveals in the affectionate courtesy of his refusal, but because it is believed to have been the last letter that Mr. Boston wrote:

'My Very Dear Sir, –
I am obliged downright to acquaint you that I have been of a considerable time, and am still, in an apparently dying condition. All business is quite over; and I can no more, as matters stand, correspond with any about MSS. or anything else, but must leave them to the Lord, and the management of my friends as he shall direct them. I do not doubt but your God, who has seen meet to row you into deep waters, will, in due time, bring you out again; but there is need of patience. I cannot insist. The eternal God be your refuge, and underneath the everlasting arms, and plentifully reward your twelve years of most substantial friendship. – I am, my dear Sir, yours most affectionately,' etc.

On the 20th day of May 1732, and in the fifty-sixth year of his age, within the brief period of a fortnight after he had preached, from the window of his manse, his second sermon on the necessity of self-examination, Thomas Boston died, as has been happily said, scarcely old in years, but weary with labour and meet for heaven. There was no lingering on the brink of the great river. It happened according to his wish and his prayer, that he might end his work and his life together. It is a comforting fact to the children of God that in every instance our heavenly Father not only appoints the fact, but also the time and the manner, of their death. When Jesus foretold to Peter his death in old age, and by crucifixion, we are informed, in the inspired narrative, that he did this, 'signifying by what death he should glorify God'. We are thereby assured that 'all our times are in his hand'; and that while the manner in which his redeemed ones are removed from the world may be very various – some dying under great and prolonged suffering, with 'pains and groans and dying strife', others with peace and even triumph, as if they felt themselves already in the everlasting arms – there is a Father's wisdom and love in them all, even in the most unlikely and mysterious. Ralph Erskine died with the cry of 'Victory, victory' upon his lips. The dying words of Andrew Fuller were, 'I have no raptures, and I have no fears, but I have such a faith as I can plunge with into eternity.' Mr. Scott, the learned and pious commentator, was vexed for a time by Satanic temptations and assaults, though, in the end, he could thank God for victory and unclouded hope. The great missionary Schwartz turned his death-bed into a pulpit, and, surrounded by native Indian princes, charged them, as if with his last dying words, 'See that none of you be wanting from the right hand of Christ at the day of judgment.' Henry Martyn, one of the most devoted and self-denying missionaries of his times, died alone in the sandy desert, with not so much as one friend to hold up to his parched lips a cup of cold water, or to close his eyes. And now this saintly pastor of Ettrick has his prayer answered, that he might end his life and his work together, and that death might be to him almost as if it were without dying.

'Oh that without a lingering groan
I might the welcome word receive,
My body with my charge lay down,
And cease at once to work and live!

'No guilty doubt, no anxious gloom,
Shall damp whom Jesus' presence cheers;

My light, my life, my God is come,
And glory in his face appears.'

Thomas Boston of Ettrick was a great man; great in the sense in which John the Baptist was great, by his consecrated life, in which he glorified God and did good to men – 'great in the sight of the Lord'. We have only to look back upon the narrative we have given of his life in order to attest our judgment. We think of him in his young ministry at Simprin, where, by means of it, in the course of seven years, the universal ungodliness and indifference among its people were supplanted by a living faith and holy conduct, so that 'the wilderness became a fruitful field'. We next behold him in Ettrick, with its much larger sphere, in which, when he entered on it as its minister, he found profane swearing, neglect of public worship, and impurity in some of its worst forms among the prevailing habits of its parishioners; and these, after many years of earnest toil and 'prayer ardent which opens heaven', yielding at length to the might of the gospel which he preached, and Ettrick becoming 'a fruitful garden of the Lord'.

There next arises before us Mr. Boston's writing and publishing his 'Fourfold State', which, during several generations, was more used of God for the conversion of men than any other book of human composition, not only influencing an individual here and there, but bringing whole counties in Scotland, containing all classes and conditions of men, under its divinely transforming influence. It was like 'a lamp from off the everlasting throne which mercy brought down'. Next came the 'Marrow' controversy, in which Mr. Boston and the other Marrowmen did battle with various forms of error, especially seeking to deliver the gospel in all its divine fulness and freeness from the restraints and barriers which human ignorance and self-righteousness had placed around it, even suffering rebuke and shame for their fidelity to Christ in seeking to remove every obstruction from the fountain of life. Through all those years of grievous wrong and persecution, Mr. Boston stood firm, even when, as once happened, he stood alone. The truth is, that there was the spirit of martyrs in this true minister of Christ; and if he had lived a hundred years earlier, in the days of the Covenanting struggle which at length won for Scotland her civil and religious liberty, we feel sure he would have been ready, if need be, to walk with firm step to the martyr's stake.

Then came the closing years of Mr. Boston's life, which, as far as his failing strength permitted, were much employed in the preparing and publishing of books which seemed to have been called for by the doctrinal necessities of the times, such as his treatises on the Covenant of Works and the Covenant of Grace, and his Notes on the Marrow. Shall any one say that the man whom God had so eminently gifted and used as his willing instrument in bringing myriads into his kingdom, and defending the faith once delivered unto the saints, was not in the highest sense a great man – 'great in the sight of the Lord'? We shall not shrink from affirming, that in some attainments he stood supreme among the great men of his time; and one who was well qualified to judge, not long since gave it as his opinion that Thomas Boston was 'the best Hebrew scholar in Scotland *in his day*, and that he was also the freshest and most powerful of Scottish living theologians'.[1]

How interesting it has been to witness the deep and tender affection shown by the people of Ettrick for their afflicted minister in the closing months of his life, as disclosed in the scenes which have been described in an earlier part of this chapter. It was no superficial sentiment of shallow sympathy which produced such tokens of regard. No doubt these had their root, in part, in the case of many, in their gratitude to him through whose faithful guidance they had been led to the feet of Jesus and into the way of life. Nor could they forget his unfailing sympathy with them in all their times alike of sorrow and of joy. And their love had also sprung, in no slight degree, from that saintly life which he had lived before them, and which testified to the divine reality of his faith. The daily witnessing of such a life as his was like reading a bright page in Evidences of Christianity. There was therefore a veneration towards this man of God which had something in it more than love.

---

1. Dr. James Walker, author of 'Theology and Theologians of Scotland'.

Long, indeed, before he died, the name of Boston had become a cherished household word in every home in Ettrick. It was a kind of synonym for sanctity. And the children in those simple homes had been taught to love him and to pronounce his name with reverence. And anecdotes regarding him, and many of his remarkable sayings and pointed proverbs, were repeated and treasured in those homes, and had even come to be circulated in regions far beyond Ettrick, and in due time transmitted from generation to generation. An eminent bishop of the Church of England was accustomed to speak of Philip Henry as 'the sweet saint of Nonconformity'. Why may we not speak of Thomas Boston as the sweet saint of Scottish Presbyterianism? In our thoughts we would place his name on the same roll of Scottish saints and worthies as that of Samuel Rutherford a hundred years before – the pastor of Ettrick and the pastor of Anwoth.

It was not long, however, ere the summons came which called Mr. Boston hence; and it was only then that his stricken people knew how much they had loved him. What a Bochim must all Ettrick have become on that saddest of days when the messengers bore to every home the tidings of their beloved pastor's death! 'Know ye not that there is a prince and a great man fallen this day in Israel?' And what a funeral, composed of multitudes with deep unfeigned grief, stretching far beyond the churchyard wall, who had come to lay in the grave the precious dust! Heaven had already opened its golden gate to receive his immortal spirit; and his many converts who had ascended to glory before him had hastened to welcome him in. And as the mourners approached to look for once into the narrow house, would they not seem to hear a tender voice calling to them from above, 'What is our hope, or joy, or crown of rejoicing? Are not even ye in the presence of our Lord Jesus Christ at his coming? For ye are our glory and joy'?

'I heard a voice from heaven saying unto me, Write, Blessed are the dead which die in the Lord from henceforth: Yea, saith the Spirit, that they may rest from their labours; and their works do follow them.'

13

SUPPLEMENT

It is pleasant to be able to add to our narrative a pen-portrait of Mr. Boston, evidently written not long after his death, by his three most intimate friends and fellow-workers in the ministry of the gospel – Messrs. Colden, Davidson, and Wilson. They have thus twined together a beautiful wreath, and laid it on his grave:

'Mr. Boston was of a stature above the middle size; of a venerable, amiable aspect; of a strong and fruitful genius; of a lively imagination, such as affords what is called a ready wit, which, instead of cultivating, he laid under a severe restraint; of tender affections; a clear and solid judgment; his temper candid, modest, cautious, benevolent, obliging, and courteous; had a natural aversion to anything rude or uncivil in words or behaviour, and a delicate feeling in meeting with aught of that sort; could be heavy and severe in his words, where there was just occasion, or he judged the same necessary.

'He was early called by divine grace; all along afterwards exercised unto godliness; walked indeed with God, in all his ways daily acknowledging him; frequent in solemn, extraordinary applications to Heaven (namely, upon every new emergent of duty, difficulty, or trial), followed with evident, comfortable, and confirming testimonies of divine acceptance and audience; a judicious observer, recorder, and improver of the dispensations of divine providence, in connection with the Word, his own frame and walk, and consequently of great experience in religion.

'He was accurately and extensively regardful of the divine law in all manner of life and conversation, even in things that escape the notice of the most part of Christians; of a tender conscience, carefully watching against and avoiding the appearance of evil, compassionate and sympathizing with the distressed, charitable to the needy; a dutiful husband, an indulgent father, a faithful and an affectionate friend, to which he had a particular cast in his temper, which proved a rich blessing to those who were favoured with his friendship.

'He was a considerable scholar in all the parts of theological learning, and excelled in some of them. What he was for a humanist, even toward the latter end of his days, his translation of his own work on the Hebrew accentuation into good Roman Latin will abundantly testify; was well seen in Greek; and for the skill he attained in the Hebrew, he will, we are satisfied, in ages to come, be admired and had in honour by the learned world, especially when it is understood under what disadvantages, in what obscurity and seclusion from learned assistance, the work was composed; and when it is considered how far, notwithstanding, he has outstripped all that went before him in that study, namely of the Hebrew accentuation. He understood the French; and, for the sake of comparing translations, could read the Dutch Bible. There were few pieces of learning that he had not some good taste of. But all his knowledge behoved to be otherwise discovered than by professing it.

'He was a hard student, of indefatigable application, so that whatever he was once heartily engaged in, he knew not how to quit, till, by help from heaven and incessant labour, he got through it. He had a great knowledge and understanding of human nature, of the most proper methods of addressing it, and the most likely handles for catching and holding of it. He had an admirable talent for drawing a paper; was an admirer of other men's gifts and parts, liberally giving them their due praise, even though in some things they differed from him; far from censorious, assuming, or detracting. As a minister, he had on his spirit a deep and high sense of divine things; was mighty in the Scriptures, in his acquaintance with the letter, with the spirit and sense of them, in happily applying and accommodating them for explaining and illustrating the subject. His knowledge and insight in the mystery of Christ was great; though a humbling sense of his want of it was like to have quite sunk and laid him by, after he began to preach. He had a peculiar talent for going deep into the mysteries of the gospel, and at the same time for making them plain, making intelligible their connection with and influence upon gospel holiness, notable instances of which may be seen in his most valuable "Treatise on the Covenants", and in his "Sermons on Christ in the form of a Servant".

'His invention was rich, but judiciously bounded. His thoughts were always just, and often new; his expressions proper and pure; his illustrations and similes often surprising; his method natural and clear, his delivery grave and graceful, with an air of earnestness, meekness, assurance, and authority tempered together. No wonder his ministrations in holy things were all of them dear and precious to the saints. He was fixed and established upon solid and rational grounds in the Reformation principles, in opposition to Popery, Prelacy, superstition, and persecution; was pleasant and lively in conversation, but always with a decorum to his character, quite free from that sourness of temper or ascetic rigidity that generally possesses men of a retired life. He fed and watched with diligence the flock over which the Holy Ghost had made him overseer; and notwithstanding his eager pursuit of that study which was his delight, he abated nothing of his preparation for the Sabbath, nor his work abroad in the parish; nor did he so much as use the shorthand whereof he was a master, but always wrote out his sermons fair, and generally as full as he preached them. Far from serving the Lord with that which cost him nothing, it was his delight to spend and be spent in the service of the gospel; was a faithful and, at the same time, a prudent reprover of sin; was imbued with a rich measure of Christian wisdom and prudence, without craft or guile, whereby he was exceedingly serviceable in judicatories, and excellently fitted for counsel in intricate cases. Zeal and knowledge were in him united in a pitch rarely to be met with.

'He had a joint concern for purity and peace in the church; no man more zealous for the former, and, at the same time, more studious of the latter, having observed and felt so much of the mischief of division and separation; was exceeding cautious and scrupulous of anything new or unpresented, until he was thoroughly satisfied of its necessity and ground. It was his settled mind that solidly and strongly to establish the truth was, in many cases, the best, the shortest, and most effectual way to confute error, without irritating and inflaming the passions of men, to their own and to the truth's prejudice: on all which accounts he was much respected and regarded by not only his brethren that differed from him, but generally by all sorts of men. To conclude, he was a scribe singularly instructed unto the kingdom of heaven, happy in finding out acceptable words – a workman that needed not to be ashamed, rightly dividing the word of truth; a burning and a shining light. The righteous shall be had in everlasting remembrance.'

Along with this skilfully discriminating and affectionate estimate of Mr. Boston, prepared by his three lifelong and most endeared friends, it will not be unwelcome to our readers that we here introduce his graceful and modest estimate of himself:

'That cast of temper whereby I was naturally slow, timorous, and diffident, but eager in pursuit when once engaged, as it early discovered itself, so I think it hath spread itself all along through the whole of my course. It hath been a spring of much uneasiness to me in the course of my life, in that I was thereby naturally fond where I loved. Yet I cannot but observe that my God hath made a valuable use of it, especially in my studies, combating natural difficulties therein, till surmounted by his favour. Agreeable unto it, I was not of a quick apprehension, but had a gift of application; and things being once discovered, I was no more wavering in them. I was addicted to silence, rather than to talking. I was no good spokesman, but very unready, even in common conversation; and in dispute, especially at a loss when engaged with persons of great assurance; the disadvantage of which I often found in Ettrick, where an uncommon assurance reigned.

'The touching of my spirit so as to be above fear, the moving of my affections and being once well dipped into the matter, were necessary to give me an easy exercise of my faculties in these and other extempore performances. My talent lay in doing things by a close application, with pains and labour. I had a tolerable faculty at drawing of papers; yet no faculty at dictating, but behoved to have the pen in my own hand, and even in that it would often have been a while ere I could enter on. Accordingly, as for my sermons, it was often hard for me to fix on a text; the which hath often been more wasting and weakening to me than the study of a sermon thereon. I studied my sermons with the pen in my hand, my matter coming to me as I wrote, and the bread increasing in the breaking of it. If, at any time, I walked, it was occasioned by my sticking. Meanwhile, it would frequently have been long ere I got the vein of my subject struck; but then I could not be easy unless I thought I had hit it. Hence it was not my manner to shift from text to text, but to insist long on an ordinary, the closing of which at length I readily found to relish as much with myself and the serious godly as the other parts preceding.

'Thus, also, I was much addicted to peace and averse to controversy; though once engaged therein, I was set to go through with it. I had no great difficulty to retain a due honour and charity for my brethren differing from me in opinion and practice; but then I was in no great hazard neither of being swayed by them to depart from what I judged to be truth or duty. Withal it was easy to me to yield to them in things wherein I found not myself in conscience bound up. Whatever precipitant steps I have made in the course of my life, which I desire to be humbled for, rashness in conduct was not my weak side. But since the Lord by his grace brought me to consider things, it was much to my exercise to discern sin and duty in particular cases, being afraid to venture on things until I should see myself called thereto. But when the matter was cleared to me, I generally stuck fast by it, being as much afraid to desert the way which I took to be pointed out to me. And this I sincerely judge to have been the spring of that course of conduct upon which Mr. James Ramsay did, before the Commission anno 1717, in my hearing, give me the following character, namely, that if I thought myself right, there would be no diverting of me by any means.

'I never had the art of making rich; nor could I ever heartily apply myself to the managing of secular affairs. Even the secular way of managing the discipline of the church was so unacceptable to me that I had no heart to dip in the public church management. What appearances I made at any time in these matters were not readily in that way. I had a certain averseness to the being laid under any notable obligation to others, and so was not fond of gifts, especially in the case of any whom I had to deal with as a minister. And Providence so ordered that I had little trial of that kind. I easily perceived that in that case "the borrower is servant to the lender".'

POSTHUMOUS WORKS

In the course of our biography of Mr. Boston, we have taken notice, with more or less fulness, of the greater number of those books which were written and published by him during his lifetime; of course giving to his 'Fourfold State' its rightful and unquestioned prominence. Our work, however, would not be fitly ended, if we did not devote a supplementary section to some statements regarding his posthumous works, which were very considerable alike in number and in value, so that when any new volume appeared it was sure to be welcomed by thirsty readers far beyond the hills and glens of Ettrick.

His earliest posthumous work which came to break the silence, was his Exposition of the well-known Shorter Catechism of the Westminster Assembly of Divines, which for so many years was to hold an honoured place in the Christian homes and parish schools of Scotland. It has been usual to speak of the Catechism as 'milk for babes'; but parts of it have been found to be strong meat for full-grown men, and hence the greater need for such a commentary as the good Ettrick minister supplied. It was edited by Mr. Boston's eldest son, who was minister of Oxnam, and afterwards of Jedburgh; and the editorial work was done with rare delight and filial devotedness and reverence. It was a large and solid book of two volumes. It consisted of a series of sermons, in which usually a separate exposition was given to each question and answer, thus ranging over the whole field of popular theology.

Two parts of it are especially elaborate and valuable, and they occupy a considerable portion of the whole work. We refer to the exposition of the Ten Commandments, with the questions about 'what is required' and 'what is forbidden', and the 'reasons annexed'; and to the exposition of the Lord's Prayer, in which is laid open that rich and inexhaustible mine of devotional thought and feeling, whose words are more frequently on the lips of men than any other part of the inspired Word. It is not too much to say that the thoughtful reading of Mr. Boston's Exposition would be sufficient of itself to make a man a good theologian. And if the reader complains that there are some things in it hard to be understood, even after reading Mr. Boston's notes, let him be reminded that it is good mental discipline when, in the reading of a book, he is sometimes obliged to pause and think.

There was also a class of Scripture passages which drew forth Mr. Boston's exegetical gifts, and wrought upon his mind with a powerful fascination. We have found at times, when travelling through a country, objects and scenes which arrested our attention, and made us stand still for a time and look – the placid stream holding up its mirror to the firmament; the garden by the roadside which opened suddenly upon our gaze with its fragrance and its flowers; the foaming cataract; the mountain, green to the summit, and almost seeming to touch the sky. And there is something similar to this in the Holy Scripture. Every part of the Bible has indeed its value; but there are some portions which have a peculiar attractiveness, just as one star differeth from another star in glory – such as those which are the glowing utterance of divine compassion, or reflect the heavenly beauty of Christian morality; the incidents in the life of Jesus; his parables, which at once instruct the understanding and touch the heart, and enrich the memory with heavenly treasures; and the gleaming outbursts of a joy that is unspeakable and full of glory. It was in such passages of Scripture that our preacher often found his congenial texts; and when he found them, he lingered over them, returning to them from week to week, and discovering in them new thoughts and spiritual meanings; loath to leave them,

'Ever in their melodious store,
Finding a spell unfelt before.'

We shall mention some of those passages of Scripture which supplied to Mr. Boston the theme of many sermons, and which at length found their way, in a succession of posthumous volumes, to the public. Among others, there was the great and all-embracing gospel call which had been a favourite from his youth, and, along with 1 John 5:11, became the motto and keynote of his ministry – 'Come unto me, all ye that labour and are heavy laden, and I will give your rest.' It took many sermons to exhaust this mine, with its riches more precious than gold. He lingered long in it, like the bee in the flower laden with honey.

Luke 18:18-28, which was entitled, 'The rich youth falling short of heaven', was the theme of many spirit-stirring sermons more numerous than its verses. It did not so much sound the gospel trumpet as the trumpet of alarm; but there was mercy hidden under those expostulations and warning, which have been happily described as 'the loud rhetoric of God's love'.

Isaiah 9:6, 7, which is, perhaps, the most sublime prophecy of the Messiah spoken and written by that greatest of the prophets, 'Unto us a child is born, unto us a son is given: and the government shall be upon his shoulder; and his name shall be called Wonderful, Counsellor, The mighty God, The everlasting Father, The Prince of Peace.' Almost every word in this grand prophecy supplied the text for a sermon, beginning with the humble birth of the wondrous child, and ending with his ascent to his mediatorial dominion and glory. There was a mighty attraction to Mr. Boston in such a paragraph. As he studied it, he must have felt like one ascending from the earth on the steps of a golden ladder until he reached the summit, and, looking in, beheld, seated on heaven's loftiest throne, the Prince of Peace.

There was yet a third class of Mr. Boston's posthumous sermons which were published at a considerably later period, near to the close of the century, and which were received by Christian readers with grateful welcome. These consisted mainly of sermons preached on great sacramental occasions, both in immediate connection with the observance of the Lord's Supper and on subsidiary occasions both before and after the holy communion, such as Fast Days and Thanksgiving Days. Those were occasions in Mr. Boston's life as a minister of Christ in which he was lifted above himself. The sacrament itself, with its sacred emblems; the grand evangelical texts on which, with studied variety, he and his brethren were wont to preach; the presence of the people in great and sympathizing multitudes, stimulated at once his gifts and his graces, so that he often acknowledged with adoring gratitude that these had been to him as days of heaven upon earth. There were also sermons to the sick, the bereaved, and the sorrowful; and it is easy to understand how, when, many years afterwards, they were read by his people who had heard them preached, they were delighted to have their old impressions revived, and once more seemed to hear the sound of those lips into which grace was poured.

And we feel it to be a duty and a delight to place on the list of Mr. Boston's posthumous writings his Memoir of himself, which was not so much written by him as the fruit of recollection, but as the record of experiences just as he had beheld or lived them. It was designed, primarily at least, for the benefit of his children, and was dedicated to them in an address of much tenderness, holy wisdom, and felicity of expression, which concluded with these words:

'Labour for the experience of religion in your own souls, that you may have an argument for the reality of it from your spiritual sense and feeling; and cleave to the Lord in his way of holiness (without which ye shall not see the Lord), his work also, his interests, and people in all hazards, being assured that such also shall be found wise in the end.

'If your mother (undoubtedly a daughter of Abraham) shall survive me, let your loss of a father move you to carry the more kindly and affectionately to her in your desolate condition. Let the same also engage you the more to be peaceful, loving, and helpful among yourselves. The Lord bless each one of you and save you, cause his gracious face to shine upon you, and give you peace, so as we may have a comfortable meeting in the other world. Amen.'

What a variety of excellences in the character of Mr. Boston is unconsciously revealed in this Memoir of himself! What a life of prayer did he lead, going with his sins and sorrows, his temptations and cares, to the throne of heavenly grace! His way to the place of prayer must have been indeed a beaten path. How earnestly did he endeavour to walk according to the rule which he had laid down for the guidance of others – that of endeavouring to keep himself in a state of constant readiness for dying. And how intensely did he identify himself with the spiritual good of his people. He could have said to them, with an apostle, 'Now we live, if ye stand fast in the Lord.' He had no greater joy than to see his children walking in the truth. How charitable he was in his judgment of others; how severely did he judge himself, sometimes even treating mere infirmities as if they had been faults! How gently did he write in his diary of those who had wronged him, though he knew that its contents were sacred to himself!

We have sometimes imagined that had this man of God lived in a later century, when the cause of missions to the heathen had begun to interest the churches at home, how it would have brightened his home and his heart with a sacred joy. He would have rejoiced if he had been privileged to help in gathering in the first-fruits of the millennial glory. The tidings of islands and large portions of continents having been won to the standard of Christ would have given to him a longer and happier life, and brightened his Ettrick home, and made his face at times shine like the face of an angel. But he had a work to do which stood in close relation to the missionaries of the gospel of Christ. His mission had been, more perhaps than that of any other man of his age, to save the gospel which the missionary was to preach, from perversion and corruption. Especially in the conflicts connected with the 'Marrow' controversy, he had proclaimed a gospel which had a voice of mercy for every human being on the earth. He had set his face as a flint against those who sought to narrow its invitations to a favoured portion of the human race, and against others who burdened it with so many conditions as to surround the fountain of life with barriers, or substituted in its place its counterfeit, or so explained the glorious gospel as in the end to explain it away. In this way he had helped to preserve the gospel, and to get myriads to inscribe on their standard the motto of the 'Marrow' and of the Marrowmen – nay, the motto of Paul and all the other apostles – that the gospel was 'God's deed of gift and grant to mankind sinners of the whole human race.' To have done this was not to have lived in vain.

Christian Focus Publications

publishes books for all ages

Our mission statement –

STAYING FAITHFUL

In dependence upon God we seek to help make His infallible Word, the Bible, relevant. Our aim is to ensure that the Lord Jesus Christ is presented as the only hope to obtain forgiveness of sin, live a useful life and look forward to heaven with Him.

REACHING OUT

Christ's last command requires us to reach out to our world with His gospel. We seek to help fulfill that by publishing books that point people towards Jesus and help them develop a Christ-like maturity. We aim to equip all levels of readers for life, work, ministry and mission.

Books in our adult range are published in three imprints.

Christian Focus contains popular works including biographies, commentaries, basic doctrine and Christian living. Our children's books are also published in this imprint.

Mentor focuses on books written at a level suitable for Bible College and seminary students, pastors, and other serious readers. The imprint includes commentaries, doctrinal studies, examination of current issues and church history.

Christian Heritage contains classic writings from the past.

For a free catalogue of all our titles, please write to
Christian Focus Publications Ltd
Geanies House, Fearn,
Ross-shire, IV20 1TW, Scotland, United Kingdom
info@christianfocus.com

For details of our titles visit us on our website
www.christianfocus.com